Power of the Creed

Optimism as a Way of Life

By James M. Rankin

10th Anniversary Edition
Revised and Expanded

Power of the Creed - 10th Anniversary Edition
Copyright © 2011 James M. Rankin
Printed in the United States of America

Limited Edition

Library of Congress
Catalogue Card Number Pending
ISBN 978-1-4566-3264-9
Left Brain/Right Brain Publishing, Inc.
9096 Jamaica Beach
Galveston, Texas 77554
(409) 370-9975
james@lbrbpub.com

Typesetting/Design by Jo Landers - www.jolanders.com
Cover Design by Octavio Tierranegra
Edited by Jacki Kirsch - jkirsch418@yahoo.com

In 1912 a prolific new self-help author by the name of Christian D. Larson published one of his most influential books, entitled *Your Forces and How to Use Them*. It contained several italicized lines on one single page that transformed millions of people for almost an entire century. That one page held twelve lines of such incredible power that Optimist International still uses it as their motto for inspiration and motivation. James Rankin, a Texas entrepreneur and author of many books, saw such a rich depth in Larson's lines that he decided to write his own book about them called the *Power of the Creed*. Taking each line as a springboard into a new chapter, Rankin has written ten insightful essays of his own, each bringing added life to the wisdom of Larson's original messages. The result is thoughtful, inspiring, motivational, soul enriching and mind expanding. Rankin did well. I think Larson would not only approve, but also enjoy and even benefit from *Power of the Creed*.

— Joe Vitale, co-author of *The Secret*

Acknowledgements

It is hard to believe that it has been ten years since the publication of *The Power of the Creed*. It has indeed been a real joy to share with Optimists all around the world the genius of the Optimist Creed author Christian Larson. His writing and wisdom is the foundation for this book. Over the years many people have gone through the Philosophy of Optimism workshops that I have conducted at the International conventions and have commented that the small changes in their attitudes have made a huge difference in their business, community and personal lives.

Adopting Optimism as a way of life is the initial objective of an Optimist member. It is my heartfelt belief that if each of us can share this compassion with our fellow man our organization would be the largest fastest growing civic organization in the world.

I want to thank a few people who have been instrumental in the construction and distribution of the *Power of the Creed*. Jo Landers for her talent in the typesetting of this project along with Jackie Hirsch in the editing of the book. A special thanks to Ed Finn, Past International Vice President, for getting the organization to put Power of the Creed into the PGI program, and for his diligent commitment to building our organization. Also, I would like to recognize Past Governor Craig Kelley who was the first Governor to invite me to his district meeting when I felt the love and appreciation from the great people of Mr. Larson's home state of Iowa. I would like to send out a sincere appreciation for the unselfish work of our International Vice President Ron Graves who has internalized the creed in his life.

I hope that you will read, study and absorb the important message in this book. I want to invite you to read a few of my other works pertaining to the power of optimism including *Living the Creed*, which has been translated into Chinese and French. My newest novel is entitled *The Source of the Shining Light of Optimism*.

May you grow into the person that you always dreamed of becoming in your life. As Emerson taught many years ago that a thought is the seed of an action, so I hope that you will enjoy the Power of the Creed 10 Year Edition and the result of that endeavor will create positive momentum for your life that will materialize into something of true beauty.

Other Works by James M. Rankin

The Magic of Method Selling
Living the Magic
Inner Renaissance Rediscovered
Poems from the Spirit of Hope
Dawning of the Day
The Philosopher Poet
Power of the Creed
Living the Creed
The Source of the Shining
Optimism, A Life Enriching Philosophy
The Cherished Fruit
The Poet's Rhyme
Sun, Sand and Saltwater Poetry Collection

Coming Attractions

The Collection of Short Stories and Plays
The Power of the Creed for the Sales Pro
The Power of the Creed for the Financial Professional
Living the Creed for the Teen

Table of Contents

21 Days to a Positive Mindset

The Scrolls

Introduction

I would like to introduce to you a great friend and author, James Rankin. James is a electrifying speaker that keeps his audience in the palm of his hand. His inspirational sessions from his books *Living the Creed, The Power of the Creed,* and *Living the Magic* are shared from the heart. It is hard not to go away inspired and uplifted by sharing his passion for the Optimist Creed. James will make a tremendous difference to your Optimist District meetings or Regional training sessions.

Craig Kelley
Past Governor
Certified Trainer Board

How often we hear that one became a member of Optimist International once they read the Creed. Now in his book, James Rankin magnifies each Tenet of the Creed as a guide to live by.

Ed Finn
Past Governor
Executive Vice President for Optimist International

When I was first introduced to Optimism I was intrigued by the Optimist Creed. It was motivational, and when I recited it the words recharged my spirit, mind and body. I could not wait for Wednesday at noon so that I could see and read the creed hanging on the banner. Little did I realize that I could use the creed each and every day of my life. Many people remind themselves of the importance of the creed by adding the creed to their surroundings. The creed has been seen on a mouse pad at work, or a desk plaque, or a framed copy on the wall. Many people will read it and comment on it. It gives you the opportunity to share with them the power of the creed.

It is important for you to learn the power of P3. P3 is to personalize the creed, profess the creed, and proclaim it to others.

Personalizing the creed means that you memorize the creed word for word. When you are alone you can personalize the creed for yourself. This is a very powerful technique to assimilate the information. You have to do this exercise with a certain amount of conviction.

For example, when you recite the creed it would sound like this:

Power of the Creed

I Promise

I will be so strong that nothing can disturb my peace of mind.

I will talk health, happiness and prosperity to everyone I meet.

I will make all my friends feel that there is something in them.

I will look on the Sunnyside of everything and make my optimism come true.

I will think of the best, work for the best, and expect only the best.

I will be just as enthusiastic about the success of others as I am about my own.

I will forget the mistakes of the past and press on to greater achievements of the future.

I will wear a cheerful countenance and give every living creature I meet a smile.

I will spend so much time to the improvement of myself that I have no time to criticize others.

I will be too large for worry, I will be too noble for anger, I will too strong for fear, and I will be too happy to permit the presence of trouble.

James Rankin

Twenty-One Days to a Positive Mindset

Day One

The possibility of a new life molded and shaped entirely by you.

The powerful saying that, 'hope springs eternal', is the starting point of all progress in one's life; the idea that you have the power within your grasp to change any aspect in your life is a revelation. The famous psychologist Abraham Maslow wrote, 'Everyone has a natural inclination for self improvement.' You can be a more positive person which means you can be, without a shadow of a doubt, a healthy, happier and richer person. You have the authority to chart a new course in your life which will open up unlimited possibilities for you, but it starts with a commitment to yourself. As the Optimist Creed begins its life changing tenets for an optimistic philosophy of life, 'Promise Yourself', which means set and maintain a dedicated pattern for your life. Manage the functions of your life, which includes a daily focused positive mindset. As we quickly go through the twenty days together, do not let the simplicity of the written words drift by, rather siege it with both hands and examine it with your reasoning capabilities that you have been blessed with and absorb this life enhancing ideology.

Questions for Growth:

1. Is it possible for me to be a more positive person? ____

2. Do I feel worthy to be a more positive person? _____

3. How would my world change if I were a more positive person? _____

   _____

4. Am I willing to pay the price to be a more positive person? _____

Day Two

What does a positive life look like?

Think about what a positive life would entail from an objective vantage point. How would a person's appearance be different from the rest of humanity? Physically I would imagine that a positive person would have a cheerful disposition on their face. In other words, there would be a big smile that would enhance their appearance dramatically. They would carry themselves just a little higher with more poise, and they would walk with a sense of purpose. Now it is time to start our journey to a more positive mind set beginning with a mirror. I want you to go find a mirror and look into it deeply. What do you see? Write down your observation as though you have never seen that face in your life. Record the first thing that comes to mind as you review this reflected face. Let's go back to the place where you picked up this book. Read what you wrote down. Do the words capture the image you saw? I want to show a unique technique that will give you a glimpse into this life changing philosophy. Go back to the mirror, but this time I want you to look for something beautiful. There are so many possibilities for clues to beauty no matter who you are. I met a young lady who was a burn victim; she had the most sparkling eyes I have ever seen. What do you see now? Is it the color or texture of the skin, is it the shape of the face, is it the hair, eyes or mouth that you find beauty? It is there, you see you get what your mind focuses on, and now your mind is focused on finding beauty. You are a beautiful person in so many ways, just take a look in front of you.

Questions for Growth:

1. Do I see the beauty in life? _____

    _____

2. What do I expect from the world? _____

    _____

    _____

3. How do I expect people to treat me? _____

    _____

    _____

4. What do I expect to feel today? _____

    _____

    _____

Day Three

How would a positive life benefit me?

We are so fortunate to live in this day and age for the simple reason that you are the latest evolution of man. You are the latest and greatest edition of this species called mankind. In addition, man's advanced knowledge has supplied us with evidence and research proving conclusively that having a positive mindset would elevate your life dramatically starting with your life expectancy. Studies have proved that optimistic people live seven years longer than their negative counterparts. According to Dr. Leonard Poon, an authority on centenarians, "They score high on optimism and are rarely depressed." In fact, centenarians are one of the fastest growing segments in our culture. In 1940 the US Census listed 4,000 citizens over age 100, today there are over 50,000. Optimists are less likely to have hypertension, digestive problems, and heart disease. Dr. Christopher Peterson proved in his study that pessimistic persons were twice as likely to develop infectious diseases as Optimists. Everyone has these three dimension in their lives; however, so people only operated on a third of their capacity which means they are living just physically, or mentally and even a few on a spiritual level. When you put all three dimensions to work; you will be on a secure, strong and safe foundation for living your life. Your mind gives you the desires of your heart, your body assists you in materializing those desires into their physical equivalent with your actions, and your spiritual life keeps you inspired to follow through and to tap into the finest qualities of your life.

Questions that you need to ask yourself are as follows:

1. How is my physical health? _____

2. How is my emotional health? _____

3. How is my spiritual health? _____

4. How would being more positive improve these areas of my life? _____

    _____

5. What can I do today to ensure that I maintain a positive mindset? _____

    _____

Day Four

A Confidential Self Assessment:

Ralph Waldo Emerson wrote, "The sign of mental health is the disposition to see good in everything."

It is critical for your life to see the best that is possible in every situation you are involved in.

Mr. Emerson gave us additional wisdom with words to live by when he wrote,

> "To Laugh often, to win the affection of children, to earn the appreciation of honest critics, and endure the betrayal of false friends, to appreciate beauty, to find the best in others, to leave the world a bit better, whether by a healthy child, a garden patch, to know even one life has breathed easier because you have lived. This is to have succeeded!"

Could you imagine for just a moment what kind of world we could live in if everyone took that definition of success to heart? Think about the change in your inner world if you were to dare to embrace optimism as a fundamental core philosophy in your life. Let's do a check up to see how you fair in the category of optimism.

I constructed a test of optimism which consists of ten questions, and a simple matrix that will help you to identify your dominant attitude.

Rank yourself from 1 to 4. One means, 'not at all like me' two means, '50/50', three means, 'There are times when that may be me' four means, 'That is totally me'.

Optimism Self Test

1. I subscribe to Murphy's Law that whatever can go wrong usually will go wrong.
    1   2   3   4
2. I have the need to control everything in my life.
    1   2   3   4
3. I believe that problems are a permanent part of life.
    1   2   3   4
4. I believe that there is only one right way to do things.
    1   2   3   4
5. Outside circumstances play a large part is affecting my emotions, attitudes and outlook.
    1   2   3   4
6. I expect my future to be bright.
    1   2   3   4
7. Problems and challenges are usually temporary.
    1   2   3   4
8. I have the ability to forget negative experiences in my past.
    1   2   3   4
9. I am open to new opportunities and experiences.
    1   2   3   4
10. I have the ability to easily forgive people who may have hurt, disappointed and wronged me.
    1   2   3   4

The formula to arrive at your results would be to add up all the questions, then subtract the questions 1-5 from the total to arrive at your dominate attitude. A score of 16-20 indicates that you are a positive optimistic person. Anything less means you need to study this book thoroughly.

Another fun test that is simple and fast would be to draw a line horizontally across the page. Draw another line vertically down the middle of your first line. Write the word **Temporary** on the left side of the horizontal line, and on the right write the word **Permanent**. Now on the top of the vertically line write the word **Control**, and on the bottom of the vertical line write the word **Non-Control**. It is time to rank yourself. On a scale from one to ten ask yourself these two questions. Do you view life's challenges as permanent or temporary? Do you feel the need to control everything in your life, or can you exercise non control in situations? Now let us review the answers. If you were a person who needs to control everything and view life's problems as permanent you have been classified as a **Pessimist**. If on the other hand, you view life's problems as temporary, yet you need to control everything; you would be classified as a **Skeptic**. If you view life's problems as permanent, yet you don't need to control everything; you are classified as a **Realist**. Conversely, if you view life's problems as temporary, and you don't have the need to control everything; you are classified as an **Optimist**. Let's drill down for deeper insight. A pessimist's personality trait always looks for the possible negative outcome in every situation. They expect the worst, so consequently they are not disappointed. The skeptic's trait differs in the fact that they know things change, but unfortunately they don't adapt to the change. They tend to be moderately negative. The realist's personality trait observes life's problems as permanent. With that in mind, the realist simply adapts themselves to the current situation. They are at the whim of circumstances. They don't color the world black or white, negative or positive. The realist is under the spell of acceptance of the outside world. The Optimist is uniquely different from the rest because they see the world's challenges as temporary. They also know that there are only two possible adaptive strategies that can be used in a challenging situation. They can change the situation that exists at that moment in time, or they can choose to change themselves. Is it always possible to change the situation? Hardly, many times things are what they are; but Optimists know that they can also choose to change themselves. Which makes the most sense most of the time? The Optimist sees the challenges as temporary, so changing the situation has only a temporary effect. Yet, when the Optimists change themselves, it can be a permanent meaningful change. In addition, it is an easier process to change oneself than to attempt to alter a situation that is already in motion.

Questions for Growth:

1. What is my style for temperament? _____

    _____

    _____

2. What style do I want to develop? Why? _____

    _____

    _____

3. What is the style of the most important person in my
    life? _____

    _____

4. How would assisting them in becoming more positive
    improve the quality of both of our lives? _____

    _____

    _____

Day Five

A well balanced life is the recipe for good health.

A positive mindset is balanced in all areas of life. There are six areas of life I want to cover with you. They are as follows: **Financial, Physical Well-being, Spiritual, Family, Mental,** and **Relationships**. I have listed these items in a horizontal format for you with numbers ranging from 1, which is the lowest you would rate yourself, to 10, which is the highest you would rate yourself in each area of your life. The logic behind this exercise is to give you a clear picture of what areas you need to work on. When you are finished rating yourself, I want you to have a solid mass of mountains on your page.

	Financial	Physical	Spiritual	Family	Mental	Relationships
10						
9						
8						
7						
6						
5						
4						
3						
2						
1						

Remember that everyone who is on the peaks of their life were at one time in the valleys. Now you can assess where you are so you can begin to get to where you want to go. Strive for balance because logic should reveal that what good is a brilliant mind if you don't use it? Furthermore, what good is having great wealth if you don't have the health to enjoy it? What good is health if you don't have anyone to enjoy it with? What good are relationships if you don't have a strong family unit for those special times of need and encouragement? What good is family if you don't have the assurance of an everlasting life with them for all eternity? Remember the wisdom of a fellow Texan and thirtieth President of the United States Lyndon Baines Johnson, "We seek a nation where the meaning of man's life can match the marvels of his labors."

Questions for Growth:

1. What is the most important area in my life that I need to work on today? _____

2. How much balance do I have in my life right now? ___
   _____

3. What will this chart look like in 28 days? _____
   _____

4. Do I expect to see positive changes in my life starting today? Why? _____
   _____

Day Six

Attitude is the luxuriant for a quality life.

It is time to review your life to demonstrate how our attitudes affect our lives. The formula that you utilize would be the **ABC**'s of potential which are **Action, Behavior** and **Consequences**. Emerson wrote that thoughts are the seeds of action. The initial action is a mental one for all, for everything that has a physical form starts its existence as an invisible thought impulse. In fact, your existence started with a parent's thought, then a single cell ,then what you have seen in the mirror. The action of thoughts, followed by your behavior gives rise to the consequence of the process. Now think about an event in your life that was negative. Replay the event in every detail.

Questions for Growth:

1. Describe the event in detail: _____

   _____

   _____

2. How were you responsible for the outcome of the event?

   _____

3. Could there have been a different outcome? _____

   _____

4. What were the lessons that you learned from the event
   at the time? _____

   _____

Day Seven

The screen of the mind is the canvas
for the physical life.

Replay negative events. Now it is time to introduce you to your imagination. You have been using your memory up to this point in your progress. The imagination is defined as a conscience idea or mental picture that has not been materialized in the physical world. The imagination can be stimulated instantly simply by visualizing something in your mind. It is a right brain function, so think about the event again in your mind. Now it is your turn to rewrite the script to say what you didn't say, to do what you didn't do, to accomplish what you didn't accomplish. However, this time you are using your newest most valuable asset which is a developing positive mindset.

Questions for Growth:

1. Describe the altered event in detail. _____

    _____

2. How has the event changed? _____

    _____

3. List the different behaviors that were used to improve
    the situation and the rationale behind the change in the
    consequences of the event. _____

    _____

4. How can you put this wisdom to work in the future?

    _____

Day Eight

Empowering the mind against the enemies.

Today we are going to identify negative emotions in your life, so let me introduce you to some of the culprits to your positive mindset, mainly fear, anger and depression. These dark emotions can be tracked to the philosophy of pessimism. Pessimism is the attitude of expecting the worst possible result in any situation. Pessimism is very much like a dark cloud that hides the rays of the sun. It creates a chill in the air that forces individuals to retreat. It destroys progress in its tracks and thrives in chaos. Pessimism is the antagonist of optimism. Pessimism is clothed in negativity, which acts like a cancerous cell that seeks to dominate the mental mechanism. Negativity bullies happiness, drives out creativity, impedes energy, and dwarfs momentum. It hungers for tension. Psychiatrist Nathaniel Branden wrote, 'An emotion is the psychosomatic form in which a person experiences his estimate of the beneficial or harmful relationship of some aspect of reality to himself.' He points out that emotions really are a value response to the world that gives an individual the opportunity to exercise their own values to life events. Napolean Hill identified six negative emotions which impact the mental health of every human being and they are: anger, fear, greed, hate, revenge and superstition. The secret is to replace a negative emotion with a positive emotion. The positive emotion would be Enthusiasm, Faith, Generosity, Hope, Love, Respect, Romance and Understanding to name a few. The Optimist Creed addresses each of these negative emotions in the tenets. Remember the wisdom of Mr. Larson who wrote, 'There is nothing in your life that you cannot modify, change or improve when you learn to regulate your thought.' This will be listed at the end of this chapter.

Questions for Growth:

1. How do you overcome negative emotions? _____

   _____

2. What is the one dominate negative emotion in your life? _____

   _____

3. How can you transform it into something of beauty?

   _____

   _____

4. How could you change the environment of your home, office, retreat to become a catalyst of positive change?

   _____

   _____

Day Nine

Acting as if.

Many people are reluctant to use this very effective strategy because it appears to be insincere. It is called the 'act as if' principle and it is grounded in the premise that a person act out the characteristics that they want to possess. I like to call it a dress rehearsal to prepare for the time when the act becomes real. I really believe that Oprah Winfrey is a great talk show host because she acts like a great talk show host, Ronald Reagan was a great president because he acted like a great American President, and you will be a positive person because it starts with you acting like a positive person.

Questions for Growth:

1. Name a mentor in each of your life categories that can assist you in fully developing your potential. _____

   _____

2. Write out the characteristics of the role you will play in the future. _____

   _____

3. What does a person with a positive mindset look and sound like? _____

   _____

4. Read a book on acting; for example, *The Magic of Method Selling* or *Living the Magic*.

Day Ten

Developing Affirmations:

It is your responsibility to take charge of the thoughts that enter your mind. To focus constantly on the possibility of growth is the key to improvement. One very effective way to aid in this endeavor is to utilize affirmations.

An affirmation is a form of self-talk that assists in the reprogramming of your subconscious mind. Some of my affirmations are:

- Each day I am developing into a better, smarter and more loving person.

- I like myself because I always take constructive action to make things happen.

- I strive to be perfect because I never make mistakes knowingly.

- I am happy because I choose to be happy.

- God is beautiful, nature is beautiful, and I am beautiful.

Another important affirmation comes from Mr. Larson,

> "Think of yourself as gaining ground along all lines, as finding better and better circumstances, as increasing in power and ability, and becoming more healthful in body, more vigorous and brilliant in mind, more perfect in character, and more powerful in soul."

An even more powerful application for affirmations is to take full ownership of the desirable traits that you want to possess. For example, here are a few of my favorite ones:

- I am Happiness.

- I am Health.

- I am Success.

- I am an Optimist Person.

- I am Peace.

When you drill these statements deep down to your subconscious mind, you can't help but become the affirmation you have selected for yourself. The underlying logic is that if I am truly happiness then no one can take it away from me. Why? It is an intricate part of me as well as health, success, optimism and peace. It is all empowering when you approach each day of your life with this realization. You are what you expect yourself to be now and in the future.

Questions for Growth:

1. Write out three affirmations that you want to incorporate in your life _____

   _____

   _____

2. Schedule daily quiet times to review your affirmations.

3. Think of these new thoughts seeping deeper and deeper into your subconscious. Think of your affirmations at bedtime to accelerate the progress.

4. Write affirmations for each the important areas of your life; i.e. physical, mental, spiritual, family, financial, relationships. _____

   _____

   _____

   _____

   _____

Day Eleven

Understanding the Great Within.

One of the biggest obstacles for individuals who are attempting to make changes in their lives is the fact that they see themselves as just ordinary people with no special traits or purpose. They live with the idea indelibly inscribed in their mental makeup that they are incapable of being a positive and happy person. It is important for you to reprogram your conscience mind to the possibility that you can be a positive person. The change of attitude will require you to reprogram your subconscious mind. Christian Larson wrote, 'Who thinks constantly of the greater worth that is within him, and who tries to feel and realize his superior nature, will give quality to every impression that may enter the subconscious; and according to the law of action and reaction, will steadily develop greater quality and worth throughout his entire nature.' When you have a clear vision of what you want to be, when you commit yourself to being a positive person, when you develop the habit of seeing the best in everything, you will begin to become that which you seek: A positive individual.

Questions for Growth:

1. What is the last thing that you think about before going to bed? _____

    _____

    _____

2. Do you have an active dream life? _____

3. Do you feel that having a positive mindset could improve the quality of your dreams? _____

4. What are some effective way to reprogram your subconscious mind? _____

    _____

    _____

Day Twelve
The Power of the Will

I want to share another idea that will assist you in developing a positive mindset would be to adopt the first tenet of the Optimist Creed which states, 'to be so strong that nothing will disturb your peace of mind.' Mr. Larson taught that more people are disturbed by the world of things, which is the external side of life, the weaker is our will. When we strengthen our will the probability of maintaining our peace of mind is greatly enhanced. The stronger our will, the more control we will exert in our physical and emotional being. Mr. Larson emphasized the power of the will by outlining the functions of the will which are as follows:

- The will to initiate
- The will to direct
- The will to control
- The will to think
- The will to imagine
- The will to desire
- The will to act
- The will to originate ideas
- The will to give expression to those ideas

- The will to will into action any of those ideas
- The will to employ the highest and most perfect action of any force faculty in the mind.

When you develop a strong iron will, you have created a force that will propel you in the direction of your objective, which is to be a more positive person. In addition, as you develop your will you will acquire what Christian Larson taught, 'He works in the conviction that he must, can and will succeed, because he has the power; and it is the truth—he does have the power—we all have the power. To live, think and work in the conviction that there is more of you within the real depths of your being, and to know that this more is so immense that no limit to its power can be found, will cause the mind to come into closer and closer touch with this greater power within, and you will consequently get possession of more and more of this power.' This is all made possible with the ability to believe.

Questions for Growth:

1. How aware are you in the development of your will?

   _____

2. Do you believe you can strengthen your will to obtain a positive mindset? _____

3. How would a stronger will help you accomplish your goals? _____

   _____

4. Cite an example of when you used your will to change a situation: _____

   _____

5. Who do you know who is strong willed? Give an example of their experience: _____

   _____

Day Thirteen

Embracing your inner self.

This is day of celebration for you have reached the two weeks mark. You should be sensing your inner change as you incorporate these ideas into your daily life. The by-product of the journey that we are taking together is to create a positive mindset that will serve you all the days of your life. The fact that you have made a commitment and are sticking to it improves your self esteem, which is an essential ingredient to a positive mind set. Self esteem is defined by Stanley Coopersmith in his book, *The Antecedents of Self Esteem.*He artfully crafts a perfect definition of self esteem when he writes, 'By self esteem we refer to the evaluation that the individual makes and customarily maintains with regard to himself; it expresses an attitude of approval or disapproval, and indicates the extent to which the individuals believes himself to be capable, significant, successful, and worthy. In short, self esteem is a personal judgment of worthiness that is expressed in the attitudes the individual hold toward himself.' Your positive mindset is centered on your healthy self esteem. Self image is what you see when you view yourself, self esteem is how you feel about what you see. As I mentioned, you have demonstrated to yourself that you are a responsible person by fulfilling your obligation. Secondly, you have established a purpose for your life to be more positive, which improves your self esteem. Next, you have discovered the truth that is derived from being positive which means you will see the beauty in life, you expect to get the best out of life, and you have the ability to interpret any outcome to your positive mindset perceptive. Lastly, you will have a sense of acceptance of yourself as a good, decent and worthwhile individual who is deserving of health, happiness, prosperity, and the love from others.

Questions for Growth:

1. What have you accomplished that you are most proud of in your life? _____

    _____

2. What have you recently done that demonstrated your personal integrity? _____

    _____

3. What have you recently done that demonstrated personal initiative in any phase of your life? _____

    _____

    _____

4. Do you accept yourself unconditionally as a person deserving of everything good and wholesome in life? ___

    _____

Day Fourteen

Mastering the Mystery of Faith:

The mystery of faith has fallen off the landscape to the demise of our culture. Our current culture has become very negative and seems to relish in bad news and misfortune. That is why it is essential that you develop the faith that you can have a positive mindset. Faith is most commonly associated with religion, yet faith should be part of everyone's core belief system. If you did not possess even an inkling of faith, you would not be reading this small booklet. Your progress begins and is ensured with the fortification of faith that you can become a positive person. Faith is a rare trait; the more you exercise the habit of faith, the more faith you will attain. The stronger your faith, the more you increase the probability for your success. Faith gives you a peek into a future yet formed.

Questions for Growth:

1. Describe a time when you exercise faith in your endeavors _____

   _____

   _____

2. What area in your life do you have the most faith in? Detail these endeavors. _____

   _____

   _____

3. How can faith make accomplishments easier for you?

   _____

   _____

4. Describe your life in ten years in vivid detail _____

   _____

   _____

   _____

Day Fifteen

The cornerstone of change is Habit:

The key to a positive mindset is to get into the habit of thinking of the best possible outcome in every situation in life. In my book, *Power of the Creed* I examine the advantages of adopting Optimism as a philosophy of life. The word Optimism is derived from the Latin word Optimum which means the very best. The Optimist Creed, written by Christian Larson and published in his book entitled *Your Forces and How to Use Them*, in 1912 introduced this unique creed that was adopted by Optimist International in 1924. The creed provides a guild post to maintaining a positive mental state of mind. Aristotle said it best, 'We are what we repeatedly do; therefore, excellent is not an act but a habit.' I like to say if you sow a positive thought, you will reap a positive action, so when you sow a positive action, you reap a positive habit, when you sow a positive action, you reap a positive life. Get into the habit of filling your mind with the powerful, positive and possible that will inspire to greater heights in your life.

Questions for Growth:

1. What is your automatic response when things don't go your way? _____

    _____

    _____

2. How do you start your day to ensure a positive mind-set? _____

    _____

    _____

3. List three positive habits that have served you well. If not, what three habits would you like to develop that will potentially serve you well? _____

    _____

    _____

4. What negative habits do you need to replace? _____

    _____

    _____

Day Sixteen

Expectancy.

Expectancy focuses on the optimum outcome that can result from any situation that one finds himself in. With that in mind, optimism begins with the hope that the goal will be realized. So that is why you need to know what you want, so you can use expectations to increase your chances of reaching your goal. If you don't know where you are going, then any road will take you nowhere. You are right. When a person knows what they want, they are in a better mental position. Expectancies becomes your personal path blazer for you and your objective. This belief states that expectancy magnetizes a thought. The thought then attracts the desire or objective into the person's sphere of possibility. The process for this doctrine will work for you, but you will need to follow these instructions. First, you need to have an idea of what it is you want in a situation or in a macro sense in life. Think about it deeply and often. Broaden the idea to encompass a larger range of time. How will this idea enhance your life and others? Then write it down clearly in a journal, so that you can read and reflect on it. Next visualize yourself going through all the necessary functions in order to obtain your objective. When you are in the situation that you have planned out, then act as if the objective has already been realized.

Questions for Growth:

1. What does an expectant attitude look like to you? __

   _____

   _____

2. How could using this idea improve the quality of your life? _____

   _____

   _____

3. What are you expecting to happen in your life right now? _____

   _____

   _____

4. Do you expect to have a positive mindset? _____

   _____

   _____

Day Seventeen

Interpretation.

Another step closer to your positive mindset is to understand the power derived from the ability to use interpretation in your life. This doctrine is grounded in the knowledge that every action is open for interpretation. Every individual has the legitimate right to decide for himself the merits of any situation. This principle empowers you to convert a situation to your own level of optimism. The doctrine of interpretation enables you to replay any event in your mind to explain in your own terms what took place. Optimism states that there is something of value in all human endeavors, no matter how tragic the results might seem at the time. Optimism provides the lenses through which to see the good in everything. Interpretation involves the technique of viewing all undertakings with an objective eye. Reserve judgment of an action until it has been filtered through a process of optimism. As the word translation is defined, so too are the situation's activities revealed to you. Optimism allows you to express, in another attitude, the happenings of your world while retaining the actual event. The process begins with the subjective point of view. This type of interpretation is found to be limited to one's own desires and is flawed with immediate gratification.

Questions for Growth:

1. What was the worst thing that ever happened to you?

    _____

    _____

2. What was the after effect from the event? _____

    _____

    _____

3. What lessons did you learn from the event? _____

    _____

    _____

4. How did you respond to the event with your life experi-
    ence? _____

    _____

    _____

Day Eighteen
Meaning.

As you begin to develop a positive mindset, it is important that you ground it with strong unwavering meaning in your life. Everyone should be reaching for something outside themselves. I believe it was the American astronaut John Glenn who said that everyone needs a 'basis of convictions and beliefs so strong that they lifted individuals clear out of themselves and caused them to live and die, for some aim nobler and better than themselves.' In order for optimism to be a workable philosophy in your life, you need to have meaning attached to your life. So I need something that will get me out of bed in the morning. You need something that burns in your heart and dominates your thoughts all day. Yes, I am talking about a magnificent obsession. It can be anything, but you need to have something in your life besides your own physical needs. That is why materialism is such a stale state of existence. How do you figure out what it is that you want to get excited about in life? It takes time and an assessment of your interests. Life is about risk. Viktor Frankl, the founder of logotherapy, wrote, 'Man must risk committing himself to a cause not worthy of his commitment. Perhaps my commitment to the cause of logotherapy is erroneous. But I prefer to live in a world in which man has the right to make choices, even if they are wrong choices, rather than a world in which no choice at all is left to him. In other words, I prefer a world in which, on the one hand, a phenomenon such as Adolf Hitler can occur, and on the other hand, phenomena such as the many saints who have lived can occur also. I prefer this world to a world of total, or totalitarian, conformism and collectivism in which man is debased and degraded to a mere functionary of a party of the state. Having meaning in your life clearly differentiates you from all the other souls in the world. It illustrates and defines who you are and where you are going. It tells the world what you value and what you will defend on this earth. Meaning is important in my life. People with some kinds of mental illness have a vacuum of meaning in their lives. Having meaning would give me a sense of purpose. It will increase your motivation for living.

Questions for Growth:

1. What is your most dominate passion? _____
   _____

2. Is there anything in your life that you would lay your life down for? _____

3. How can you use that passion in everything you come in contact with in the course of your life? _____
   _____

4. What are you giving back to the world in which you live in? _____

Day Nineteen

Understanding the Nature of Love.

This element of a positive mindset has a transforming quality to it that will ensure the attainment of your objective. The element is the condition of love that states that every living thing in the universe has a purpose. With that in mind, all things should be treated with respect and dignity. Love is an extension of the spiritual nature of man. Love is not the result of an action; rather it is the cause. It is the belief that love is in all people and is released to others unconditionally. It is derived from the creator of the universe, who is in fact love. The yearning of every living person is to love and to be loved, and this fact fuels its power. It is an intricate part of all people and can be expressed in differing degrees to everyone. Under the philosophy of optimism, recognition, positive action, and a nurturing spirit for all living things communicate love. The doctrine of love consists of tolerance, temperament, and tenderness. Love is nonjudgmental of others and maintains an even temperament in all situations. It is evident that only the strongest of our kind can be tender to others."

Questions for Growth:

1. Were you raised with unconditional love? If not, describe what that meant to you in your life. _____

   _____

   _____

   _____

2. How would your life change if you incorporated love into your life's philosophy? _____

   _____

   _____

   _____

3. Can you love yourself unconditionally? If not why not?

   _____

   _____

   _____

4. Describe how you would use love in your everyday walk through life. _____

   _____

   _____

   _____

Day Twenty

Discovering the Rainbow for your face.

This is the day that the inner self is revealed by the outer self. Your positive mindset is communicated to the world without a single word spoken. The underutilized asset that you possess is your smile that shares with the world your new philosophy for life. A smile is the rainbow for the face, and it can improve any circumstance that you find yourself in. Take this little test to discover the power of this little gem of wisdom. I want you to focus on the biggest challenge that you have in your life, now put a big smile on your face. Think of your biggest disappointment in your life, now put a big smile on your face. Think of your biggest fear, now put a big smile on your face. Now think about the fulfillment of your dreams, now put a big smile on your face. A smile can make anyone's face, no matter what their appearance may look like, to improve. A smile opens doors, minds, and hearts, so make sure you use it every day of your life.

Actionable Ideas for a Positive Mindset:

1. Go to your mirror and smile big.

2. Make it a habit to smile at your family members, colleagues, and complete strangers.

Questions for Growth:

1. Were you raised in a home where everyone smiled? _

   _____

2. How often do you smile on a daily basis?_____

   _____

3. Do you see the benefits of smiling throughout your day? _____

   _____

4. Will you commit to this life changing habit today? ___

   _____

Day Twenty-One
A Positive Mindset Personified.

The amazing part of this program is that the hand that picked up this book is the same hand that will put it down; however, the mind of the person who picked up the book is not the same mind that will put this book down. This program is designed for positive changes in the mind and heart of the participant. As the Philosopher Poet wrote,

> Stretching the mind
> An idea that might bind
> A thought to a word
> A message that's heard
> Leading the world into a direction
> Onto the path of perfection.

You are discovering your path to your perfection. Orison Sweet Marden captured this thought in the early 1900's when he wrote, "We can so educate the will power that it will focus the thoughts upon the bright side of things, and upon objects which elevate the soul, thus forming a habit of happiness and goodness which will make us rich. The habit of making the best of everything and of always looking on the bright side is a fortune in itself." One of the most effective ways to maintain a positive mindset is to have a creed that you can live your life by, that provides a pattern and serves as a lighthouse for the proper maintenance of a healthly mental temperament. Christian Larson wrote the Optimist Creed in the early 1900's, and it will serve as an ideal creed for you.

Promise Yourself -

To Be So Strong that Nothing Can Disturb Your Peace of Mind

To Talk Health, Happiness, and Prosperity to Every Person You Meet

To Make All Your Friends Feel that There in Something in Them

To Look at the Sunny Side of Everything and Make Your Optimism Come True

To Think Only of the Best, to Work Only for the Best, and to Expect Only the Best

To Be Just as Enthusiastic about the Success of Others as You Are about Your Own

To Forget the Mistakes of the Past and Press on to Greater Achievements of the Future

To Wear a Cheerful Countenance at All Times and Give Every Living Creature a Smile

To Give So Much Time to the Improvement of Yourself that You Have No Time to Criticize Others

To Be Too Large for Worry, Too Noble for Anger, Too Strong for Fear, and Too Happy to Permit the Presence of Trouble

I recommend my book, *Power of the Creed* which examines the writings of Mr. Larson to expand on these life changing tenets of the creed.

Actionable Ideas for a Positive Mindset:

1. I will recite the creed everyday for the next twenty-one days.

2. I will read the book *Power of the Creed* to develop more insight into this historic piece of self improvement literature.

3. I will join an Optimist Club or become a friend of Optimist. (Application is located at the back of this book)

4. I will commit myself to living a positive and optimistic life.

Self Completing Sentences for a Positive Mindset.

This exercise is a very effective way for you to access your deep inner feeling in your objective to modify your mode of thinking. It is important to be spontaneous in your responds; the goal is to capture the first impression that flashes in your mind. Do not contemplate on your answers; go with your gut instincts.

1. I feel it is possible for me to _____

    _____

2. Positive possibility thinking means _____

    _____

3. When I believe in something I _____

    _____

4. Thinking about my positive life makes me _____

    _____

5. When I was young I thought_____

    _____

6. When I look into my own eyes I see _____

    _____

7. Those times when I expect the best I _____

    _____

8. When I focus on the best I feel _____

_____

9. I think that I will live _____

_____

10. When the subject of religion comes up I _____

_____

11. I describe my attitude as _____

_____

12. It comes natural for me to _____

_____

13. I am most comfortable when _____

_____

14. The first thing I do when things get tough is to _____

_____

15. Ever since I was a child I wanted _____

_____

16. Being a positive person means _____

_____

17. What I want more than anything else in life is _____

_____

18. I define negativity as _____

_____

19. What challenges me the most in life is _____

_____

20. Happiness to me means _____

_____

21. Health to me means _____

_____

22. Wealth to me means _____

_____

23. Other people think that I _____

_____

24. My legacy will be _____

_____

25. I give back to society by _____

_____

Power of the Creed

Congratulations on your accomplishment of becoming a new poised, positive, powerful person; however, this is not merely a diet, it is a life time philosophy. Review the steps if you are ever tempted to fall back into old negative habits. You are a new person with new expectations and new interpretations of life's events. It is time to make your mark on the world and the wonderful people that inhabit it. I want to leave you with a unique thought written by Ram Dass', 'In that invulnerable inner place, We come to know what it is each of us that can never be lost, and can never die. We find at last, in our own hearts, The source of all happiness. We find the dwelling place of Love. We find the home of our loved ones, Both living and dead. We find our Self.' That self is one that you have created for yourself infused with the life changing power of a positive mindset secured and steadied with the philosophy of Optimism. As Mr. Larson reminds us all, 'Our destiny is not mapped out for us by some exterior power; we mapped it out by ourselves. What we think and do in the present determines what happens to us in the future.' When you equip yourself with a positive mindset you will be prepared to meet any obstacle or challenge on your journey and surely overcome it to reach your goals. It will be a much more enjoyable experience with a positive mindset that does not rely on outside stimulus to maintain its existence. You are indeed a new person with unlimited potential in every area of your life, and unlimited opportunity for love.

James Rankin

Power of the Creed

Many great achievements have been accomplished by the inspiration of the written word. Words are the physical manifestation of thoughts. Words allow the spirit to touch the human ear with its melody. Words have the potential to enlighten, encourage, and energize others into action.

One of the most powerful collections of words is contained in the Optimist International Creed. This unique creed is recited hundreds of thousands of times each year by Optimists throughout the world. Christian Larson, a forerunner in the self-improvement movement, wrote the Optimist Creed in 1912. The amazing aspect of the creed is that once it is internalized, change will appear as if by magic. The words will take root in the deep reservoir of pure thoughts within you.

As your inner self is stirred, your thought patterns will begin to evolve and intensify. As Mr. Larson writes,

"Every word is an expression, and every expression produces a tendency in some part of the system. This tendency may appear in the mind, in the body, in the chemical life of the body, in the world of desire, in character, among the various faculties, or anywhere in the personality, and will work itself out wherever it appears."

Upon the attainment of a deep meaningful knowledge of the creed, you can begin to utilize it to seek improvement in every aspect of your life. It has been said that repetition is the mother of all learning. With that in mind, it is recommended that you recite this powerful creed for one month. First, repeat it in the morning as you wake up. This practice will allow you to program your conscious and subconscious, so that you can take control with the first thought of the day.

Next, recite it over lunch as you partake of your midday meal. Lastly, before you retire take a few minutes and think about the words, and more importantly, the meaning behind the words.

The objective for this book is to share with you the wonder of the creed, and to tap in on the genius of the man who wrote the creed more than eighty-eight years ago. There are ten tenets that will be covered throughout this booklet. In addition, each tenet will be examined carefully and thoughtfully to shed light on the deep and profound meaning of this classic piece of self-improvement literature.

It is my heartfelt belief that with an understanding of the creed, you can begin to apply its wisdom in your daily life. The fruits from this endeavor will be health, peace of mind, and joy, which will flow in your life and the life of those special people who share your life.

Mr. Larson believed that if men and women would begin to cultivate their own greatness buried within each person, we would have an entirely different world. There are a few in all cultures who have elevated the world to higher levels. These people are called Optimists. Mr. Larson longed for this to be an intrinsic part of all human beings. He asked, "If he did, would we not, in another generation or two, witness unmistakable evidence of the coming of a new and superior race, and wouldn't strong men and women become far more numerous than ever before in the history of the world?"

It is not a choice; it is a responsibility that each of us has as a member of this human team, to reach inside of ourselves and emerge with the best that is in each of us. Herbert Spencer wrote, "There is a principle which is a bar against all information; which is proof against all argument; and which cannot fail to keep a man in everlasting ignorance, best expressed as the only obstacle to your growth. This principle is contempt prior to examination." Open your mind to the power of the creed.

— James Rankin

James Rankin

Promise Yourself

In this fast-paced, mass-communicated, over-communicated society, we have the tendency to lose touch with our inner self. Conversely there are more ways of getting in touch with others than have ever existed since the beginning of time. You could make a phone call, send a letter, fax, page, email, telegram, or even make a personal visit. The important question is how do you get in touch with yourself. The creed starts off by addressing that very issue. Promise yourself to follow these tenets to live out your true potential.

You begin your journey with a commitment to yourself. You should be grounded in the security and the expectancy that you will grow into something of great value to your world as you embody the knowledge instilled in the creed. Many people have never stopped for even a brief moment to observe the observer, to step back and view themselves with an objective eye. Most people don't take the time to determine what and who they are, or what they want to become in the future. It is important to get to know yourself. As Shakespeare wrote many years ago, "To thine own self be true, and it must follow as the night to day, thou canst not then be false to any man."

To enrich the lives of others, you must enrich your own

life. It is important for you to love yourself sincerely. I am not referring to an egotistic attitude of self-grandeur, but one of respect and acceptance. This is accomplished when you set aside a certain time everyday to spend alone.

Many people use a variety of means to recharge their battery and center themselves that can include meditation, prayer, or yoga. Changing your habits to include time with yourself should be a priority as you begin to form your new way of life.

In St. Exupery's book entitled *Wind, Sand & Stars*, he writes,

> "Perhaps love is the process of my leading you gently back to yourself". That is where love must begin if it is going to have an impact on others. Take care of yourself in all areas of your life, which encompasses your physical, mental, and spiritual well-being."

These three dimensions of man entail the maintenance and upkeep of the physical body, the development and education of the mind, and the purification and focus on your inner spirit. Our modern society has attempted to quench the spiritual nature of man. This has had a devastating effect on our communities, and especially on the youth of this generation. As Christian Larson wrote, "When the soul is not awakened, consciousness lives in a condition of spiritual death and mental darkness.

The mind is deprived of the guidance of the spirit, and

therefore follows blindly the changing desires of the flesh, those desires that are suggested by the world of things. In consequence, the person is almost buried in materiality, and goes wrong more frequently than otherwise, usually not knowing the reason why. The result is sickness, trouble and adversity, or the sum total of the ills of life. The real cause of all these ills is spiritual death, and the great, infallible remedy is the spiritual life. The ills of life are produced by the mind going wrong, but the mind will not go wrong when it is led by the spirit, and the mind invariably is led by the spirit when we live in the life of the spirit."

It is not my intention to focus entirely on the spiritual nature of man; rather you should balance all areas of your life. It is quite apparent that the spiritual life of man is the moral compass, which can dictate our thoughts and actions. Throughout your reading I will share various writings from Christian Larson to enhance your understanding of these ten tenets.

As we continue to progress into the meaning of the creed you will clearly see your path to enlightenment through the fog. As Mr. Larson illustrates,

"There is no reason whatever why any person should continue to have a weak body, a weak character or a weak mind; anything in the being of a man can be made strong if the subconscious is properly directed to bring forth the greater life and the greater power".

The fundamental truth, which makes all of these tenets work for you, is an unwavering faith. Faith begins with yourself and spreads to everyone you come into contact with.

Mr. Larson writes, "Faith is the hidden secret to everything; the key that unlocks every door that may exist in the universe; faith is the perfect way to that inner world from which all things proceed; faith is the royal path to the unbounded power, immeasurable wisdom and limitless love; faith is the gate ajar to that kingdom which first must be sought if all other things are to be added; faith is the hidden secret to every desire and need of man."

Promise yourself to have faith in the power of faith as you learn the tenets of the creed.

Questions for Empowerment

1. Are you comfortable being alone?

2. How do you feel when you reach your objectives?

3. What is something that you are committed to?

4. How do you relax when you are experiencing stress?

5. Describe your best attributes.

Scroll I
New Beginnings

I stop for this moment of time to reflect on the journey ahead. I stand now in the middle of the symbolic fork in the road. I want to choose the right path, the right way, and the right life from now on. It will require me to open my mind and my heart and to listen to a new voice, which will lead me in the direction of my dreams. As I see myself in my mind's reflection, I see the young boy with eyes so wide as well as, the old man deep in experience. Both of these roles are parts of me—the past, present, and future. My past is a memory for learning, the future is my promise, and the present is my life. I realize that my life is now filled with chaos and darkness. I desire order and light that will transform my life into a peaceful existence. My old ways for living will now be turned into ash. I will hold the ashes in my hands briefly before I throw them over the mountainside. I watch the ashes floating on air before they disappear into the depths of the Earth. So too will my old desires, appetites, and attitudes dissipate. My mental plane is emptied out and is ready to be filled with wisdom. Just as a mason lays his brick one at time, just as the masons have for two thousand years, so too does this wisdom stand the test of time and is in fact timeless.

Each brick of wisdom serves as a foundation for me, and each brick reminds me to live each day fully. I desire a new life and a new beginning. I long to be whole and enlightened.

James Rankin

Tenet I

To be so strong that nothing can disturb your peace of mind

The first tenet reinforces the notion of not letting the world influence your thinking. To maintain a positive mental attitude and peace of mind is a prerequisite to a quality life.

How do we gain peace of mind? In the classic best seller, *The Power of Positive Thinking,* Dr. Norman Vincent Peale states:

> "The essence of the secret lies in a change of mental attitude. One must learn to live on a different thought basis, and even though thought change requires effort, it is much easier than to continue living as you are. The life of strain is difficult. The life of inner peace, being harmonious and without stress is the easiest type of existence. The chief struggle then in gaining mental peace is the effort of revamping your thinking to the relaxed attitude of acceptance of God's gift of peace."

Christian Larson taught us that we all have peace of mind. However, very few people experience this peace. The true strength of an individual is mental toughness. It has been said that it is not what happens to you that counts; rather it is how you choose your behavior in the situation that tells the tale. If you stop for a moment and realize how much control you can exercise in every situation you face in your life, you will be amazed. There exists a small gap between what is called the stimulus and the response. Think back.

What if you had waited and reflected just a few moments before you reacted to someone or something in your life? How might the event been changed?

We all have free will to pick our own course of action in all of our situations. William James, the father of modern psychology, was quoted as saying, "My first act of free will is to believe in free will." Human beings have too long been conditioned to react to events in life.

There are really only two options available for anyone in life when confronted with any situation. You can respond or react to the event. When you respond, you are drawing the positive forces to you. On the other hand, when you react, you literally repel the solution to the problem.

The choice is yours. Inner strength is a by-product of healthy, constructive thoughts, and is an important ingredient in maintaining your inner strength. When you evolve into a person of inner strength, you will begin to develop a firewall between you and the world; which will protect you against the arrows of negativity. It doesn't necessarily matter what the situation is; rather it is your attitude during the situation that makes the difference. When you look at every challenge as an opportunity for growth, it will make a difference in your life. Remember the words of James in the Bible who wrote,

> "Consider it pure joy, my brothers, whenever you face trials of many kinds, because you know that the testing of your faith develops perseverance. Perseverance must finish its work so that you may be mature and complete, not lacking anything." It takes effort initially to function with that type of mindset, but the rewards are worth the time that you invest in your new attitude.

Dr. Wayne W. Dyer wrote in his book *Pulling Your Own Strings,*

> "Being strong in no way implies being powerful, manipulative, or even forceful. By operating from strength, I mean leading your life from the twin positions of worth and effectiveness."

As the term implies, you determine your self worth. How do you really view yourself? Ask yourself if you spoke to your friends the way you internally speak to yourself, would you have any friends at all? The greatest mental distress people experience often comes from their own mouths. In order to be so strong that nothing will disturb your peace of mind, you need to embrace the concept of contentment. Contentment is not defined as the lack of ambition; rather it is the acceptance of a certain moment in time. It is a pre-requisite to peace. Be all you can be right now.

When you experience contentment, you will control all of your anxieties about the uncertainties of the future. You can be immersed in the very essence of life, which is this tick of time. As Mr. Larson writes,

> "The great secret of secrets is to live your own life in your own world as well as you possibly can now. Be what you are today. Do not be satisfied to be less than you can be today and do not strive to be more. Progress, growth, advancement, attainment, these do not come through overreaching. The mind that overreaches will have a reaction; the person will fall to the bottom and will have to begin all over again. Real attainment comes by being your best where you are just for today, by filling the present moment with all the life you are conscious of; no more."

The present moment is a gift. What you do with your life should be a gift back to others and to your creator. Mr. Larson continues,

> "To live the purest, the largest, the fairest, the most useful, the most beautiful, and the most spiritual

life possible just for today. To be our very best here and now, with no desire to outshine some other beings, but simply to be all that we can be now to fill the present moment with all the spiritual sunshine that we can radiate through the crystal walls of love, peace, faith and joy; and to live so near to the supreme that we may touch the hem of his garment whenever we so desire. This is life, and he who lives with such a purpose forever in view, shall never know an undesired moment."

The key to living the truth of the tenets is to approach this wisdom with an open heart and mind. You need to fill yourself with the expectancy that these ten tenets have the potential to change your life for the better.

These tenets will help you mine the greatness that is dormant in you, and bring it in full face with your world. You are in charge of what you allow in your mind. With that in mind, make sure you screen everything that enters into the greatest miracle of nature, your own mind. When you begin to live out the truths expressed so brilliantly by the master Optimist Christian Larson you will possess the gift of peace, which will fortify your strength to not allow anything to disturb your inner tranquility.

Questions for Empowerment

1. What is it that seems to always upset you?

2. What can you do to address & eliminate the situation?

3. What does peace of mind mean to you?

4. Do you feel that you are content at this point in your life?

5. What are some creative ways to strengthen your emotional & mental state?

Scroll II

To Be So Strong That Nothing Can Disturb Your Peace of Mind

As nature's fury swells the seas and thunders through the trees, yet my spirit remains calm and serene. For I know that I do not control the wind, rain, or hail. However, I am in charge of my inner weather. It is solely for me to choose to process the information and conditions that take place on the outside of my being. I choose to be at peace, always looking for the positive element in every situation that confronts me in life. Emerson's words still ring true today that the sign of mental health is to see good in everything. I will internalize those words and my new eyes will see good in all people and in all things. There are exceptions, and I will not fall prey to unrealistic situations. However, from my view from the mountaintop, all is well with my life. I will embrace this peace and hold it in my arms securely. I will hold it so tight that this wonderful peace will become an intricate part of who I am. I know that when this peace becomes a part of me, then no one can take it away from me. Can someone through his words remove my feet or hands? So too will it be difficult for anyone or situation to extract peace from me. I take ownership of the healing power of peace for I know whence this peace originates. My peace is derived from the very source of creation itself. With this transformation I do become complete. Its value shines like gold that is pristine and refined. My peace will not diminish for it is perpetually genuine.

Each brick of wisdom serves as a foundation for me, and each brick reminds me to live each day fully. I desire a new life and a new beginning. I long to be whole and enlightened.

Tenet II

To talk health, happiness and prosperity to everyone you meet

The second tenet is an interesting one, which encompasses many different trains of thought. First of all, we are asked to talk health. Total health is comprised of physical health, financial health, mental health, and spiritual health. It seems that if any of these is out of balance, it can adversely affect each other area.

listed below is a graph showing the area of life, and numbers from one to ten. Your job is to record where you feel you are at this stage of your life in that particular area of your life. The number ten represents that highest level you can reach in that area of your life.

	Financial	Physical	Spiritual	Family	Mental	Relationships
10						
9						
8						
7						
6						
5						
4						
3						
2						
1						

One represents the lowest level in that particular area of your life. Now simply make a point on the graph where you feel you are.

Next, connect all the dots on the graph. Now look at your creation. You will notice some peaks and some apparent valleys. Don't be troubled; many people who are on the peaks today spend some time in the valleys. The good news is that you now have a handy self-assessment tool to begin to improve those areas of your life that you may have neglected. This is your range of life goals. Dale Carnegie wrote that while in a doctor's office he observed some good advice hanging on the wall. It was entitled, "Relaxation and Recreation" and read: "The most relaxing recreating forces are a healthy religion, sleep, music, and laughter. Have faith in God, learn to sleep well, love good music, see the funny side of life, and health and happiness will be yours." That is what I call a true prescription for life. When you follow this advice everyday, you will be attracting the right circumstances to your life.

As Mr. Larson writes, "Talk health. It is the best medicine. When people stop talking sickness they will stop getting sick. Talk health and stay well. Talk health to the person who is sick and you will cause him to think health. He who thinks health will live health, and he who lives health will produce health."

What an amazing thought! This tenet contains wisdom that has been distilled to its essence. When you speak, you create and you set in motion the result of your words for yourself. With that in mind, you must force yourself to talk health instead of its deadly counterpart.

Health is a gift that you can prescribe for yourself. Remember right thinking produces right living, which leads straight to health, abundant health. Mr. Larson expounds on this point when he writes, "When disease threatens, have faith; and have faith in faith; feel the very soul of faith in every atom of your being and the healing power of the soul will fill your system through and through."

You get in life what you focus on. Mr. Larson reminds us to focus only on the very best in life and in return for this approach you will receive the very best that life has to offer.

The next part of this tenet is a fascinating combination of words, happiness and prosperity. These two items are very similar in one respect. They cannot be attained directly. Simply put, both of these items are a by-product of something else. In order to be happy, you must do something that will bring true happiness to you. Conversely, in order to obtain wealth, you must provide some type of product or service that is needed in society.

Viktor E. Frankl, in his book *Psychotherapy and Existentialism*, points out that

"the will to pleasure is really a self-defeating principle inasmuch as the more a man would actually set out to strive for pleasure, the less he would gain it.

This is due to the fundamental fact that pleasure is a by-product, or side effect, of the fulfillment of our strivings, but is destroyed and spoiled to the extent to which it is made a goal or target. The more a man aims at pleasure by way of a direct intention, the more he misses his aim."

When you strive to live to the letter of this tenet of health, wealth, and happiness, the obtainment of the latter is greatly improved when you view each of these objectives as the result of your actions. According to Christian Larson, "the real man continues to be well and strong at all times, and the life of the real man is perpetually a life of perfect health and wholeness. To live constantly in the conscious realization of the life of the real man is to always feel well, in body, mind and spirit."

This trio—the mind, body, and spirit—working together as a single unit will create a powerful force that will set in motion the materialization of your desires.

Christian Larson reminds us to, "talk happiness, and you will always remain in a happy frame of mind. You will encourage thousands of others to do the same. You will become a fountain of joy in the midst of the garden of human life, and who can tell how many flowers of kindness and joy unfold their rare and tender beauty because you were there." When you share your happiness with others you, radiate your internal joy, which reflects sunlight to those around you. Your thoughts, words, and actions represent your light.

The all-time best seller, the Bible, said it best. Jesus shared one of his many parables:

> "You are the light of the world. A city on the hill cannot be hidden. Neither do people light a lamp and put it under a bowl. Do people light a lamp and put it under a bowl? Instead, they put it on a stand, and it gives light to everyone in the house. In the same way, let your light shine before men, that they may see your good deeds and praise your Father in heaven."

Let your light shine to the world from the inside out. The message is that you are endowed with special skills of communication that allow others to experience your joy. Optimism is something that the world can never get enough of ever. Turn on your light of optimism to show others the path to attainment.

When you mentally digest the words in this tenet, you will become the person who turns the tide. You become the one who makes the difference, and changes the attitudes and perceptions of others. You become transformed into a person who becomes an asset in everything that they are involved in.

Success starts with you, and you impact others by your words. Talk happiness to everyone. Ralph Waldo Emerson wrote, "Nothing can bring you happiness, but yourself. Nothing can bring you happiness, but the triumph of principle."

One affirmation that is powerful is "I am happy because I chose to be happy." It really is that simple. True happiness originates from the inside of a person. In most cases, people expect outside stimulation will produce happiness. However, to their dismay, it is short lived, often lost shortly after the event has been completed. This mode of thought is like attempting to fill a bucket with a big hole in the bottom. It will never be full. If you expect people, places, and things to bring you happiness, you are setting yourself up for a major disappointment. The author of the creed writes, "Happiness adds life, power and worth to all your talents and powers. It is most important, therefore, that every moment should be full of joy," It is also important to share that happiness with others. In doing so, we can assist others in experiencing happiness.

One effective strategy for gaining happiness is to incorporate the "act as if" principal. This principle states that if you act out the behavior you want to possess, you will begin to feel the sensation of the new behavior. This new feeling paves the way for you to incorporate this new behavior in your life.

To attract people into your life, you should fill your language with happiness. Mr. Larson writes the prescription for friendship, "You can win ten times as many friends by talking happiness as you can by talking trouble. And the more real friends you have the less trouble you will have."

The last part of the tenet states "To talk prosperity to everyone you meet." First of all, the true wealth of an individual cannot be measured on a balance sheet in monetary terms. Rather, the true wealth of an individual is the legacy that he or she leaves behind with others.

According to Mr. Larson,

"The value of the life comes not from having much, but from being much; and happiness is invariably a state of mind coming, not from what a person has, but from what he is. We must remember, however, that he who is much will gain much, providing the powers in his possession are practically applied; and his gains will have high quality whether they be gains in the world of things or in the world of mind, consciousness and soul.

As we saw previously, wealth is a by-product of a constructive action. Your quality of life is in direct proportion to the service you provide to others. One of the most abused phrases comes from the incorrect interpretation of the scripture that states that the love of money is the root of all evil. It is not money itself, but the idolatry and worship of money that corrupts. Money is very important to society. With it churches and libraries are built; the youth are educated. Money allows individuals to experience self-reliance and freedom to live the life of their dreams.

Ayn Rand said it best when she wrote in her best seller

novel *Atlas Shrugged,*

> "So you think that money is the root of all evil? Have you ever asked what is the root of money? Money is a tool of exchange, which can't exist unless there are goods produced and men able to produce them. Money is the material shape of the principle that men who wish to deal with one another must deal by trade and give value for value.
>
> Money is not the tool of the moochers, who claim your product by tears, or of the looters, who take it from you by force. Money is made possible only by the men who produce. Is this what you consider evil?"

Money can be a benchmark that illustrates the service and value you provide to your community.

Money should work for you; you should not work solely for money. Money is a furious slave driver, but it is an humble servant. It is important to remember that money should not be an end in itself; rather it should be a natural by-product of your efforts.

Living this tenet will allow you to tap in on a force that will assist you in your conquest.

Mr. Larson understood that the repetition of words could produce faith. He writes, "Through faith every desire can be realized, and every object in view can be accomplished, because faith places mind in touch with the power that can do all things."

When you speak of prosperity often, you will eventually attract it to you. In conclusion, Mr. Larson stresses that a true optimist understands the power of words both to the speaker and the listener.

An optimist uses this information to impact his or her world in a positive way. As Mr. Larson writes, "The simplest way to use this power is to train yourself to talk the things you want; talk the things that you expect or desire to realize; talk the things you wish to attain and accomplish. You thus cause the power of words to work for you and with you in gaining the goal you have in mind." He continues, "Emphasize everything that is good in life, and the power of the Supreme will cause your words to come true."

Your success in life is rooted in the seeds of your desires that give rise to the hope that you can accomplish it. Your hope fosters your faith that you can and will be successful. Your faith generates your idealization, which in turn stimulates your imagination. Your imagination creates pictures with your visualizations, which are translated into words. Your words give life to your dreams and serve as a foundation for the completion of your goals.

Always be conscious of the words you use. Your words should be packed with the powerful, the positive and the possible with everyone you come in contact with. Words are the seeds that you plant in the minds of others, which when applied to the next tenet will bring you surprising results!

James Rankin

Questions for Empowerment

1. How do you rate each of the areas on the range of life? (See chart)

2. What is the one thing that can greatly improve the quality of your life right now?

3. Will you commit to making the necessary changes to accomplish your growth?

4. Do you have a goals program and do you track your goals daily?

5. What brings you happiness?

Scroll III

To Talk Health, Happiness, and Prosperity to Everyone I Meet

To be in perfect communion with others, I will master the art of communication. Whether to one person or two thousand people, I will learn the necessary skills to communicate a thought, idea, or concept clearly. I am aware that every time I open my mouth I create an expression, which could leave an indelible impression on others. I value this awesome responsibility, for it ushers in unlimited possibilities for the advancement of the world. The ancient words of Tacitus provide the example in which to learn this special art form: "It is of eloquence as of a flame, it requires matter to feed it, and motion to excite it, and it brightens as it burns." I will emulate the flame that has the ability to hold one's attention. Nature's flame dances with motion. So too will I learn to illustrate my message artfully through gestures to capture my audience's mind and heart. The flame crackles as it expands. So too will I develop my voice to become like a bubbling brook or a sweet melody from a favorite song. I will learn the techniques of a well-trained voice. I will utilize voice inflection to emphasize my words. I will master articulation and pronunciation to make the task of listening effortless. I will bring life to my words so that others can understand what I have experienced. My words will guide others to my level of understanding. I will become like the flame's vibrant color of yellow, red, and orange that draws others ever so near. Nature's flowers with their own brilliant colors attract the birds and the bees to feed on their sweet nectar. So too will I attract the attention of my audience with the color from my garments. My words will be reinforced with truth and passion of my subject matter. I will not use my newfound gift to mislead or misinform others for I know that a speech without sincerity is like a flower without fragrance. From this day forward I will speak with conviction and confidence. I will welcome every opportunity to share with the world about health, happiness, and prosperity. And in turn I will attract these things into my life.

Tenet III

To make all your friends feel
that there is something in them

It has been said that the best vitamin for making friends is B1. There is a lot of truth to that statement. Friendship is much like a savings account; you can't take out more than you put in. You develop friendship by first taking an interest in others. Psychologists called it being outer-directed. Many people with emotional problems have a tendency to dwell too much of their attention on themselves. Try this creative solution to your next bout with a negative feeling. When you are depressed, find someone who is less fortunate than you are, and assist him or her. Something amazing will happen; your depression will disappear! The tenet reminds us, 'to make all your friends feel that there is something in them'. In fact, you should be able to list those people whom you have taken an interest in. We should be mentoring others on a daily basis. You also need to have your own mentors who will assist you with their wisdom and experience.

The essence of the tenet is to incorporate encouragement for others. Encourage has been defined by Webster's Dictionary as, "to inspire with courage or hope and to support, and foster." In order to grow into the person whom we aspire to be we all need encouragement. Just as sunlight is essential for plant life, encouragement is equally important for human development.

Encouragement fills our personal inner reservoir that can occasionally be depleted. Encouragement is like the cool breeze on a hot summer day. It is like a second wind on the last lap of the race. It is soft, caring hands on a hard tired body. We all need to learn to encourage others.

Gandhi was quoted as saying that one finds himself when he loses himself, and you lose yourself in the service to your God, country, and fellow-man. Each of us contributes to the current emotional climate in the world. In recent years that climate has been one of complacency and apathy. I am reminded of a story of a young man from the rough side of town. When asked if he felt the world was filled with ignorant and apathetic people, he simply replied, "I don't know, and I don't care."

It is quite apparent that the moral fiber of society has been pierced. The signs are all around us with students shooting students in our public schools, national leaders not being accountable for breaking moral and national laws, and fewer and fewer people want to give of themselves to make our world a more pleasant place.

The solution to some of the world's woes is tenet three, which proclaims, "Make all your friends feel that there is something in them."

As the tenet declares, we can share our inner conviction

to perpetuate the good and the pure especially with the youth of the world. Napoleon Hill wrote, "Congratulate yourself when you reach that degree of wisdom which prompts you to see less of the weaknesses of others and more of your own, for you will then be walking in the company of the really great."

The tide of the masses still can be saved as long as we are free to express ourselves. In our present period, there are still people who live under governments that have stripped them of their basic freedom, yet there is still civil disobedience. It is our nature to be free.

The price of freedom is never free; rather, it is purchased with personal sacrifice, and diligence.

With that in mind, your association with others is not something to be taken lightly. Many people live their lives in an automatic pilot mentality, never realizing they are creating their internal and external environment. Unfortunately, the external environment influences many people too much, so pick your friends carefully. Place value on each relationship that you have with others.

On the subject of association, I am reminded of the story of an underground church in the Soviet Union under communism. The members of the church were singing their hymns when two soldiers burst in on the congregation. They stormed the front of the church and aimed their rifles at the group. They gave those who were not Christians a chance to leave before they began firing on the crowd. Many people ran for the exits, yet a few of the dedicated Christians stayed After the mass exodus, the soldiers placed their rifles down and sat down to hear the sermon. The soldiers were afraid of being reported, so they wanted to worship with only true Christians.

A similar incident happened in Littleton, Colorado, when two crazed students went on a shooting rampage that resulted in many deaths. It was reported that one of the boys asked a young girl if she was a Christian. She responded in the affirmative and was shot to death.

There are times when you must stand up for your convictions.

If you don't stand up for some truth or principle, then you can be deceived by almost anything. When you radiate truth and principle in your life, you will become a magnet to others. You will be the kind of person whom people like to spend time with. You will attract people into your life who will reinforce your sense of well-being purpose. You want to be the friend that you would want to have. One of the traits that all friends should possess is a trait that seems to have fallen from the landscape.

This trait is character. Yes, character does matter. It has been said that character is what you do when no one is looking.

Character is an important trait that all successful people possess. According to Mr. Larson, "Character in the largest sense of the term is impossible without a strong will, and it is impossible to accomplish anything that is of permanent value without character."

People of character have strong wills and are principled in their beliefs. They have a moral compass, which dictates their actions. When you are a person of character, you will command respect from others. This will enable you to inspire others to follow your directions and to assist them to greater attainments.

It is interesting to note that the traits we dislike in our fellow man are often the very ones we possess.

It was in this vein that Mr. Larson wrote,

"What you admire in others will develop in yourself. Therefore to love the ordinary in anyone is to become ordinary, while to love the noble and the lofty in all minds is to grow into the likeness of that which is noble and lofty."

The tenet in the Optimist Creed states, "To make all your friends feel that there is something in them." That something in them is the vast untapped potential that exists in every individual who has ever walked this earth.

This vast potential I am writing about was present in a young boy who designed a tic-tac-toe software program and later in life created a multi-billion dollar software company. Another example is found in a young college student who assembled computers in his dorm room and sold them by mail order. He then went on to build a billion-dollar computer company. In our rich history, there are a couple of brothers from North Carolina who dreamed of flight, and a young man with a silly toy that he designed to improve communication, and a young scientist who was not content to light his way through life with candles. Each of these men tapped into the unlimited part of themselves to discover their potential and greatness. Bill Gates, Michael Dell, the Wright brothers, Alexander Graham Bell, and Thomas Edison have created fortunes for thousands and employment for millions.

They have improved the standard of living for all of us. Each of these men heard all the reasons why his dream couldn't be accomplished, yet he found a way to fulfill it. Each one of these industrious men had someone who encouraged him and made him feel that something was indeed in him.

Mr. Larson writes, "When you meet a person who does not look well, call his attention to the sunny side of things, and aim to say something that will give him new interest and new life. You will thereby nip in the bud many a threatening evil, and carry healing with you wherever you go." Make everyone feel that there is something in him or her, and discover that there is something in everyone. Yes, there are people who have disappointed us, yet you must always remember the wisdom of Mr. Larson, who reminds us never to forget this bit of advice: "With all their defects there is nothing more interesting than human beings; and the reason is that for every shortcoming in man there are a thousand admirable qualities."

There are a few old sayings that should be dissolved from our lexicon. Sayings such as, "one more for the road", "just let it ride" and "it is lonely at the top". If you live out the truth of this tenet, you should never be lonely at the top providing you didn't use others as steps on your way up to the top.

You should take others with you. Making all your friends feel that there is something in them means that you are assisting them in their own development. It is important to realize that we need others to accomplish our own dreams. No man can do it alone, and if you can do it alone, is it really worth doing? Meaningful and great accomplishments can only be accomplished with other people.

It has been said that the mind is like a microscope in that you can only see what you focus on. What are you putting under your mental microscope? Do you focus on the possibilities or the limitations, the good or the bad, the victory or the defeat?

What you focus on is what you will get, so why think of anything else but on a positive perception about life? You will never know how a kind word can impact another person's day. Take an active interest in others, and share in their victories. One of the most valuable things that you can do for your friends is to learn how to listen. Try this next time you are with one of your friends. Don't think of anything while the person is speaking to you. Focus your entire attention on each and every word that comes out of their mouth. You will be amazed at what you find.

Listening is something that most people aren't very good at, yet it is so important to our lives. In the training of our associates, I teach them about the power of empathic listening. Empathic listening is an advanced way of communicating with others. Empathic listening forces you to concentrate not only on the words the person is using in their dialogue, rather on the feelings they are sharing with you behind the words. Becoming a good listener will attract more friends to you than even the most brilliant conversationalist. The secret is to take a sincere interest in others, share in their joys, sorrows, and their solutions to their struggles. That is what community is all about, that is what family is all about, that is what life is all about. Start caring for your fellow man, and see a whole New World bloom before your very eyes.

The wisdom of King Solomon captures the essence of this entire chapter when he wrote in Proverbs 11 :25 thousands of years ago, "A generous man will prosper; he who refreshes others will himself be refreshed." When you build up others, you are building up yourself. Share your optimism with those around you, and encourage others, so that you will bring out the best that is inherent in everyone and yourself.

Questions for Empowerment

1. Name your three best friends.

2. How much time do you spend with them?

3. Are you a good listener?

4. What have you done lately that illustrates your encouragement to others?

5. How can you be a better friend to others?

Scroll IV
Sharing the Fruits with Others

As I grow into the person that yesterday I only dreamed of, I realize that my development has taken place through my own smooth and bumpy roads, through the lives of other people, and through written words. I know that the quickest way for me to become the person I desire to be is that I must have a mentor. Just as a young lion cub observes its mother to learn basic survival skills, I need to have mentors in my life to observe their success patterns. Although I have my own unique traits and strengths, role modeling some of my weakness will strengthen all my many links in perfect alignment. I will be open to new ideas and suggestions to perfect my performance in life. Just as the sun has two directions, east and west, so too I will have a mentor and will also become a mentor for others. I will share my life with others to improve their life. It is part of nature's secret that when I teach others, then my path will become shorter to the goal of perfection. There is no greater joy than to bring a smile to a young person's face when they accomplish something in their life from hitting a ball, making a grade, spelling a word, speaking to their peers, or obtaining a diploma. You have entered into immortality when you have internalized worth and skills into the lives of others, which are then passed down from generation to generation. I desire to perpetuate my mentors, and, yes, I too desire to live forever though the lives of other kindred spirits.

Tenet IV

**To look at the sunny side of everything,
and make your optimism come true**

The next tenet reminds us to look at the sunny side of everything, and make your optimism come true. In order to live out the true meaning of the creed, it is important to adopt as a philosophy of life the theme of optimism.

One definition of optimism states that it is the preponderance of life to focus on the positive possibilities, rather than the negative ones. Webster's Dictionary defines optimism as, "a disposition to expect the best possible outcome or to emphasize the most positive aspects of a situation." The popular test to determine if someone is an optimist is to ask him or her this simple question. Is the glass half full or is it half empty? The person's reply will reflect if she views the world in positive or negative terms. The true optimist sees the glass as half full; whereas, the pessimist sees the glass as half empty. If you analyze this statement, you will find that the pessimist is taking something out of the glass. The optimist is putting something into the glass.

When you think about it, is there really any other way to live your life? Ralph Waldo Emerson wrote, "The sign of mental health is the disposition to see good in everything."

It is critical for your life to see the best that is possible in every situation you are involved in. Mr. Larson writes,

> "Hold yourself constantly in a positive, masterful attitude, and fill that attitude with kindness. The result will be that remarkable something that people call personal magnetism."

Is it realistic always to take the positive side of the equation? Does it really make a difference in the scheme of life to be positive? The answer is that being optimistic about life doesn't change the situation; rather it changes your view of the situation. Furthermore, it changes you internally to face the situation in a whole new light.

It is important to change your vocabulary to express your optimism. Listen to the way most people reply when asked how they are doing. Some of the responses I hear are, "Not bad", "Getting by", "No problems yet." What kind of expectant attitudes are reflected back to you? Tell people how you want to feel. I like to tell people "Absolutely great!"

Society needs to change the tone of our language to be more positive. I would like to hear the weatherman report that we have a sixty-percent chance of sunshine instead of a forty-percent chance of rain, or a restaurant that is always open verses never closes. In the war on drugs, wouldn't you rather say "yes" to being drug-free than just saying "no" to drugs? No is the first two letters of the word nothing.

Using positive words will empower you to take on the challenges of life boldly and courageously.

Mr. Larson advised us,

"Train yourself to face the sunshine of life regardless of circumstances. When you face the sunshine, everything looks right, and when everything looks right, you will think right. It matters not whether there is any sunshine in life just now or not. We must think of sunshine just the same. If we do not see any silver lining, we must create one in our own mental vision."

It is not always what happens to us that counts, rather it is how we respond to what happens to us.

The words of Ellen Wilcox remind us to be sunny: "Smile and the world smiles with you. Frown and you frown alone." It has been said that a smile requires fewer muscles in your face than a frown. Furthermore, a smile increases your face value ten-fold. It is interesting that in all the foreign countries I have visited a smile is understood in every language.

The natural inclination of human beings is to smile when someone smiles at you. You must consciously decide not to smile back at someone. Begin to smile more during your day and see how other people respond to you. A smile reflects to the world your optimism.

When you live out the tenets, you will see personal

growth take shape. You will realize just how essential it is to give of yourself to your community. In the early 1800's, Alexis de Tocqueville, a writer from France, came to this county to study our culture. The underlying trait that set us apart from all the other societies in the world was our voluntary civic duty, which is carried out freely by the citizenry.

One of the most important parts of our society is our youth. The Optimist Club is one of the only international civic organizations that is dedicated in the service to the development and advancement of the youth. The Optimist Club was founded in 1919 in Buffalo, New York. The original motto of the organization was "Friend of the delinquent boy," It was later changed to "Friend of the boy," and finally to its present motto "Friend of youth." This is appropriate considering Optimists work with all youth. Some of the projects include Youth Appreciation Week, Respect for Law, Bike Safety, and many other projects that promote goodwill in the community. I recommend you read the history of the Optimist captured in a book entitled *Of Dreams and Deeds.*

Optimist Clubs offer a unique opportunity for a man or woman to give of themselves and their talents to the community. In addition, it is the objective of optimists to continue the advancement of our youth. The quality and character of the members builds a camaraderie that is irresistible. The objective of the clubs is to provide an avenue for the members to develop leadership skills. An individual is limited in what she can do for a community. However, when many are united with like-minded men and women empowered by an optimistic spirit and willingness to share, there is nothing that cannot be accomplished.

The Optimist Creed has been a part of the organization almost from the beginning. Where did it come from? How did we come to embrace it as our own? Let us turn to *Of Dreams and Deeds*, the official history of Optimists International written by the late Gordon S. "Bish" Thompson (reprinted by permission of the Optimists International). Once organized, Optimists began casting about for a motto, a slogan or a creed they could live by. Many were suggested; none was quite what was wanted and needed. Though each did contain the fundamental belief of Optimists, none seemed to offer the whole philosophy concisely, crisply and completely.

In Los Angeles, California, soon after the end of World War I, Mrs. James V. Westervelt clipped a little item from a newspaper or magazine and saved it to show her husband. Jim was secretary treasurer of the Optimist Club of Los Angeles, an office of many duties including publishing the club bulletin and its yearbook, "The Disseminator." "This struck me as a fine expression of what an Optimist should try to do and be," she told her husband. "Perhaps you'd like to use it."

Jim read it over and recognized it for its worth. He reprinted it in the 1919 yearbook. He didn't know whom the author was, for in the clipping the attribution was merely "Selected." The title was simply "Promise Yourself." The little jewel of literary excellence and philosophical dynamite contained ten resolutions, ten promises a man could make to himself and which, if they were kept, would guide him constantly and dependably along the upper trail.

Los Angeles Optimists, on finding" Promise Yourself" in their club yearbook, seized it and took it for their own. Many copied it from the book and more than a few memorized it. Two years later when they journeyed north to recruit new Optimists and build new clubs in San Francisco and Oakland, they took it with them. In this pithy little document, they felt could be found all that Optimist International is and should be.

Among the Bay Area men to appreciate the creed's value was the charter president of the Optimist Club of San Francisco, "Uncle" Bert Hubbard. One of his first official acts was to have it reprinted and copies distributed among all members of Optimist clubs in the vicinity. Like Jim Westervelt before him, Uncle Bert was unable to give credit to the author.

With so many California Optimists familiar with the choice and succinct bit of prose, it was inevitable that the creed would find its way to the Optimist magazine and there it appeared—once again attributed to "Selected"—in the December, 1921 issue. Now all Optimists everywhere were exposed to it and were inspired by its simple truths.

When the next convention was called to order, in Kansas City in 1922, nearly every delegate present had a copy of "Promise Yourself" in his pocket. Hundreds of copies had been brought and distributed by Optimists of San Francisco and Oakland. Still without knowing the author, the convention adopted it as the Optimist Creed. Beginning with the August 1922 convention issue the creed became a regular feature of the Optimist magazine. No one knew who had written it but thousands knew it by heart, repeated it frequently, and made it a rule of living optimistically yet realistically. But Jim Westervelt was still curious. Who was the author of the creed now officially the Optimists' own? He did a little literary detective work and it wasn't long before he had unveiled the mystery. "Promise Yourself" appeared first in 1912 in a book titled *Tour Forces and How to Use Them*. The author was Christian D. Larson. Its theme was simply "you can do anything you want to do if you only set your heart and mind to it." It was a small volume of high inspiration and philosophy, one of many like it which began appearing on the market shortly after the turn of the century and have enjoyed popularity and wide readership ever since. All were outgrowths of the philosophy of the "Transcendentalists" of the days of Ralph Waldo Emerson, Henry Thoreau, Amos Bronson Alcott, Nathaniel Hawthorne and Margaret Fuller. You wouldn't be far wrong if you called these people the first American Optimists for they discovered, explored and demonstrated the creative power of constructive thinking.

Christian D. Larson, who was to write thirty-nine other books in addition to the one containing "Promise Yourself" and to give more than 5000 lectures, all soundly based on simple but bedrock precepts, began his career in Cincinnati, Ohio, in 1898. He lectured in public halls in the city, in homes of the suburbs and in surrounding town.

What he taught was received with active interest and enthusiasm and led to the founding of the New Thought Temple of Cincinnati. This was to become one of the largest and most successful and influential institutions of its type.

Mr. Larson was also the founder of The New Thought Temple of Cincinnati and for 25 years the editor of and chief contributor to a monthly publication called "First Eternal Progress" and later "New Progress." At one time its circulation reached 150,000 and there were subscribers in every English-speaking country in the world. While on a lecture tour to the West Coast, Mr. Larson succumbed to the climatic charms of Southern California. In 1908 he moved his home and his publication to Los Angeles. Ten years later while on a trip to Seattle, he met, wooed, and married Miss Georgia DuBois, a concert violinist. To them were born two children.

The man who gave the Optimists their Creed continued to live in Los Angeles—a near neighbor, incidentally, of the Westervelts who discovered it for them—until Mr. Larson's death in 1962. At each international convention until that time, delegates telegraphed greetings and reaffirmed their appreciation of their creed to its author.

The Optimist Creed in its original form contained twelve resolutions instead of the ten in the creed today. The two additional ones read:

> "Promise yourself to think well of yourself and to proclaim this fact to the world, not in loud words but in great deeds."

> "To live in the faith that the whole world is on your side so long as you are true to the best that is in you."

In the countless times the original writing was copied by newspaper and periodicals—usually without the author's consent or even his knowledge—both the name of the author and the last two resolutions were lost in the shuffle.

There is no accounting for the number of copies of their creed printed and distributed by Optimist International, by Optimist clubs and by Optimists as individuals, but certainly it must be up in the millions. Their creed is not to be used only by and for themselves. It is to be shared with all others and has been distributed throughout the Free World for the benefit of all. Of course, it is in every Optimist's billfold for it is reprinted on the reverse side of his membership card.

It may be seen on office desks, on the walls of homes,

everywhere it may catch the eye and speak its philosophy of optimistic living. It has been distributed among young people, given out in the streets, and sent in great number to remote corners of the globe where people are in need of a creed they can hold onto and live by. It would be pure folly to say that every Optimist lives up to his creed for that would demand perfection and no man is perfect. Likewise, it would be equally foolish to assert that men who are not Optimists cannot attain a high level of living because they do not have the creed to guide them. It may be said with conviction, however, that every person, Optimist and non-Optimist alike, who has read, considered, remembered, and made serious efforts to follow the Optimist Creed is a better person for it.

Questions for Empowerment

1. How do you define optimism?

2. How would your life change if you were to be more optimistic?

3. What recent event could have turned out better by incorporating optimism in your life?

4. Have you joined a civic organization?

5. How do you give yourself away for the betterment of others?

James Rankin

Scroll V

To Look at the Sunny Side of Everything and Make My Optimism Come True

Every day ushers in a variety of climates from the frozen snow to rain galore. However, all my days are treated as though they were bright and sunny. Although the dark clouds may hide the source of light, my Inner Light shines bright. I choose to live a life that is tempered by a mood that is balanced and always as consistent as the early morning tide. My mood steadies my ride as I pursue my objectives. The lenses through which I process my world are painted with the brush of optimism and buffer the bleak, gloomy, and dark aspects of life. They create a temporary bliss much like a soft tender kiss, which offers to turn confusion into the divine. Optimism is my philosophy, which concentrates on the positive. It always works to see that the positive becomes completed. Optimism is my shield that protects me from the world's arrows of negativity. Optimism makes the unbearable bearable, the unlovable lovable, and the impossible possible. With optimism all the things become a reality as I strive always to be focused and clear and to persist in all my worthy endeavors.

Tenet V

**Think of only the best, to work only for
the best, and to expect only the best**

It is interesting to note that as marvelous as the human mind may be, it can hold only one thought at a time. Try for a moment to think of two things simultaneously. It cannot be done. With that in mind, you must get into the habit of thinking only the best and constructive thoughts. Your most focused thoughts will inevitably materialize in your life.

As Mr. Larson illustrates, "To entertain superior thoughts is to think the very best thought and the greatest thought about everything we come into contact with." Your thoughts are the building blocks for your life.

It has been said that a human being is comprised of his or her most dominant thoughts. It doesn't matter what you are saying in your thinking; rather it is the inner power that you give your thoughts that determines their degree of success. The famous poet Thackery wrote, "The world is a looking-glass, and gives back to every man the reflection of his own face." With that in mind, create a reflection of peace, love, and joy to lift others to your place of optimism.

Force yourself to follow the tenet of thinking only of the

best possible outcome. Make sure you get into a lifestyle that starts every waking moment with a positive thought of thanksgiving for all you have been blessed with, a thought of your dreams and ambitions, a thought for the eternal life that awaits you. Just before retiring, fill your mind with wholesome thoughts to assist you in creating pleasant dreams instead of negative images, which give rise to a restless, sleepless night of tossing and turning. The advice from the master of optimism, Mr. Larson, is

> "to aid the mind in purifying itself before going to sleep attention should be concentrated upon the purest purity and the highest worth that can possibly be imagined, and to place the entire system in a state of peace, concentrate the thought of peace upon the brain center while gently drawing all the finer forces of the mind toward that center."

Sleep should be an effective tool to refresh your body, mind, and create in your soul a song. For too many people it is painful time of wishing for the dawn to break. When you own your peace of mind it will allow you to relax and fall naturally into an uninterrupted slumber and to awaken ready to take on your world.

The tenet continues to pour out the wisdom, to think of only the best. This tenet is the heart of optimism. To think of the best means to live by truth.

Mr. Larson teaches us to, "live, think, and act in the spirit of this truth, the truth that you live and move and have your being in a world of unlimited power and that through faith all of this power is placed at your command. To live in this truth, with faith, is to open the mind more and more to the perpetual influx of this power, until you gain so much of this power that nothing becomes impossible to you henceforth and forever."

Think about those words. Ponder what they mean specifically to you. Next the tenet states to work for only the best. It has been said that if you find a profession you really enjoy, you will never have to work a day in your life. Imagine spending a third of your life working on your favorite hobby. You would notice a few major changes in your overall perception of the world.

First, you would have the power of expectancy as your ally. You would look forward to going to work. Second, your energy level would increase dramatically and be sustained throughout the working day.

Third, your attitude would be more positive since you would be working on pleasant activities. Too many people chase the cool breeze on a hot summer day instead of seeking a shady place.

I am not advocating changing careers on a whim. However, if you are miserable, stifled, and unappreciated, then it only makes sense to seek out a good working environment which utilizes your God-given talents.

If your employment options are limited, then living

out the tenets can empower you to face the challenges. To think of only the best in your life, would result in shifting your mental perception about your life. Becoming an optimist will revolutionize your life in every area. In order to be optimistic about life, you must train yourself to guard against negative thinking. Here are some ideas to help improve your productivity at work. The tenet reminds us to work only for the best. It has been said that the five words of a failure are "I don't have the time," yet everyone has the same amount of time to accomplish all that is required. It is not how much time you devote to a project; rather what is important is what you put into the time.

It is a challenge to balance all the demands of the day into the twenty-four hours that make up a day. The key is not to manage the seconds of an hour; rather it is to manage yourself. I will share with you some effective ways to maximum the time that you are responsible for.

One of the most effective ways to manage yourself is to set objectives for your day. List the most important things you must accomplish that day. Put them in the proper order of importance. When you begin your day, work on that one objective until it is completed, if possible. Then proceed to the second and so on and so forth. This really is the only logical way to maximize your effectiveness.

The next suggestion is to track your productivity with a chart. By tracking your activities, you will automatically improve your productivity by twenty percent. The method is to stop every twenty minutes and write down what you accomplished.

Record any disruptions to your productivity. List the objective and the steps you went through to accomplish the stated objective. List the obstacles and roadblocks along the way, and how you overcame them. Lastly, a goals program will keep you in moving in the right direction. You need to make sure you are working on the right things at the right time. Make sure to wear your optimism as your shield, and serve as your guild.

Mr. Larson shares the differences between these different polarized sectors in the mind,

> "The optimist lives under a clear sky; the pessimist lives in a fog. The pessimist hesitates, and loses both time and opportunity; the optimist makes the best use of everything now. The pessimist curbs his energies and concentrates his whole attention upon failure; the optimist gives all his thought and power to the attainment of success and arouses his faculties and forces to the highest point of efficiency. The pessimist pours cold water on the fires of his own ability; the optimist adds fuel to those fires. The optimist is a building force; the pessimist is always an obstacle in the way of progress."

When you think a thought, you plant the potential of life for that thought. Many times we actually attract to us the very things we fear simply because we allow them to take root in the fertile soil of our minds.

One important ingredient that every successful person possesses in every type of business, sport, or entertainment industry is faith. It is important for your success to have total belief in yourself. If you are serious about the development of yourself, read carefully the wisdom from Mr. Larson,

> "Since faith is the only path to the within, and since it is only through faith that the consciousness can be expanded, faith therefore becomes indispensable to all forms of development."

All greatness in man starts with faith that good will overcome evil, that success will overshadow failure, that truth will prevail over the lie. Mr. Larson understood that the repetition of words could produce faith. He wrote, "Through faith every desire can be realized, and every object in view can be accomplished, because faith places mind in touch with the power that can do all things."

Incorporate faith in everything you come into contact with. Would you like a doctor to operate on you who didn't have the faith he had the skill to complete the operation successfully, or a lawyer who doubted if she could win in the courtroom? Why would you want to shortchange yourself by allowing doubt to sabotage your goals and aspirations? Who else beside yourself is going to have total belief in you? Conversely, if you are the only one who has this total belief, are you truly walking the walk? Results will materialize from the germination of your belief provided it is reinforced with constructive action. As Mr. Larson points out,

> "The mind that lives in doubt can see limitations everywhere; the mind that lives in faith can see no limitations, and, in fact, knows that there are no limitations anywhere. The mind that lives in doubt is in bondage to these seeming limitations, and therefore realizes nothing more of life than what is confined within these seeming limitations; but the mind that lives in faith lives in the freedom of the all of life, and is daily realizing more and more of everything that is contained in all of life. Faith can see that no matter how large or how beautiful life may be now, there is always a larger and a more beautiful life to live for, to work for and to realize in the days that are near at hand."

The classic story of Colonel Sanders reminds us never to entertain defeat. His belief was the compass that directed his ultimate success in the restaurant industry. At the ripe old age of 66, he went into the competitive business world with just his recipe for fried chicken and the persistence of a small army. The legend has it that restaurant owners turned him down hundreds of times. All that the colonel wanted was the opportunity to show that he could increase fried chicken dinner sales with his secret recipe. He wanted just a small fee for the increased sales. Years later, he found the winning combination that yielded him a personal fortune, and employment for thousands.

We all have the opportunity to experience his special blend of herbs in his delicious chicken dinners, and more importantly to use his determination as a living example for us to live our lives.

Successful optimistic living begins with the expectation that you will have a successful life. Expectancy allows action to be facilitated in a much more effective matter.

The tenet says to expect the very best. Expectancy prepares the path for your actions. Expectancy is an effective tool that you should equip yourself with in every situation you are involved in on your journey. According to Mr. Larson, "What we expect comes if our expectation is filled with all the power of life and soul, and what we believe our fate to be. That is the kind of a fate we will create for ourselves." The key words are expectation and belief.' When they are united in thought, they will bring the force necessary to accomplish your objective.

Mr. Larson continues, "When the mind expects the best and has the faith that the right will prevail, and constantly faces the superior, the true mental attitude has been laid."

You have total control over what goes into your mind. Negative thoughts produce negative results. Positive thinking increases the likelihood of positive results. That is why you need to be on guard to allow only what you want out of life into the depth of your mind, and nothing else.

Mr. Larson writes,

> "What you imagine, you will think, and what you
> think, you will become. Therefore, if you imagine
> only those things that are in harmony with what you
> wish to obtain or achieve, all your thinking will soon
> tend to produce what you want to attain or achieve."

What you do will guarantee what you will become.

Lastly, have faith you will attain and achieve all that you seek. Mr. Larson teaches us that when we incorporate faith we will magnify all abilities, skills and talents, so that what we expect will come to pass. Expectancy, the knowing of an expected outcome, is accomplished only with clear vision. Chuck Swindoll captured the essence of vision when he wrote,

> "Vision is essential for survival. It is spawned by
> faith, sustained by hope, sparked by imagination, and
> strengthened by enthusiasm. It is greater than sight,
> deeper than a dream, broader than an idea. Vision
> encompasses vast vistas outside the realm of the
> predictable, the safe, and the expected. No wonder
> we perish without it."

Vision is what every great leader has possessed since the beginning of time.

A poet wrote,

Observing the evolution of man's plight.
Absence of the seeds of desire,
Clips the wings of wonder, grounded flight
Lost life's lust as a smoldering fire.
Death of vision, end of sight.

An old, wise Indian saying said, "Begin with the end in view." Vision is essential for your success. Your vision is a picture that is triggered in the imagination, fueled by a burning desire to accomplish, molded by the power of will, and should be carried out with belief that it will be accomplished. Mr. Larson advises us, "To make every mental action constructive, and a constructive mental action is one that is based upon a deep-seated desire to develop, to increase, to achieve, to attain in brief, to become larger and greater, and to do something of far greater worth than has been done before." Incorporate this wisdom on your job and watch your results soar higher than you ever dreamed possible.

In conclusion, in order to think of the best and to work for the best, and to expect only the best, one must incorporate faith in oneself. Mr. Larson writes, "The effect of faith upon the intellect is most beneficial in every way; the reason being that the attitude of faith elevates mind above all confusion, doubt, fear, uncertainty and limitation and actually illumines the entire mental domain." When you can dismiss these negative traits from your mind, you will attain the mental image of your creation.

Jesus Christ taught over two centuries ago that, "all things are possible to him who believes." In the same way, Mr. Larson teaches each of us the simple truth that when we incorporate the use of faith in everything we come in contact with we will accomplish more. The reasoning faith is so potent is that through the use of faith we are able do all things because faith stirs that something in each of us that can and will do all things. To expect the best that life has to offer us, we must integrate faith in our lives. Many people rely only on the hope that things will work out without the power and conviction that faith can provide. Mr. Larson captures this thought when he writes,

> "Hope stands on the outside, faith walks in; hope waits to be guided, faith trusts in its own light and proceeds; hope expects to receive external help, faith awakens its own limitless power and produces results without help; hope is ever waiting for things to come right, faith goes to work and turns all things into the right; hope hopes for the best, faith lives and works in the faith that the best must come, thereby creating the best and the best only."

Arm yourself with the wisdom handed down from the ages, and own the best that is available to you.

Questions for Empowerment

1. Are you a positive person?

2. Do you work as hard as you play?

3. Are you able to control your thoughts, and concentrate your attention?

4. How would developing an expectant attitude change your family and working life?

5. What do you do exceptionally well? Can you make money doing it?

Scroll VI

To Think of Only the Best, to Work Only for the Best, and to Expect Only the Best

Wisdom has taught that man is what he thinks about all day long. Thoughts can clothe people in their own unique outfit. However, I know that I am what I do. Thought precedes an action, so I will dwell on the things that I want in life and give not a moment to the things that I don't. I will create thoughts with the intention that they will produce the best possible outcome. What I think, I will do; what I believe in, I will pursue; and what I value, I will protect. I am the sum of my life's experiences, so I choose to utilize to the best of my ability those experiences in my chosen profession. I know it is not the time I put into my work that counts; rather it is the value I put into my time. The results from my work shine a light into my true character. With that in mind, I work only for the best that I am capable of doing on the job. From this day forward, I will use the marvel of expectancy in all that connects to me. I will use expectancy to assist me in all my undertakings. I expect to be treated fairly by others, I expect to accomplish my objectives, I expect to prevail, and I expect to win. I expect the best that life has to offer me. And so I will receive the best that life has to offer me.

James Rankin

Tenet VI

To be just as enthusiastic about the success of others as you are about your own

There are two things that determine your future, what you know and what you do with what you know. It is not enough simply to think; rather, it is the actions you execute with your thoughts that count. In order to be successful you must be a person of action. Longfellow, the great American poet, wrote, "We judge ourselves by what we feel capable of doing while others judge us by what we have already done." You determine your worth by the actions you carry out each day. As Mr. Larson wrote, "The destiny of every individual to being hourly created by himself, and what he is to create at any particular time is determined by those ideals that he entertains at any time." You should rejoice for the victories of others. In order to inspire others you must be inspired. If all you have inside you is pessimism, negativity, and ignorance, then that is all you can give to others. However, if you are optimistic about the future, you truly believe in the human potential, and you feel good about yourself, then you will inspire others to realize their own potential greatness that will benefit all of society. In a world of plenty, we still have individuals who harbor a scarcity mentality.

This destructive mindset causes one to think that there are only enough resources for a finite number of people. These people envy the successes of others. They are usually not successful themselves because they spend so much of their energies worrying about others getting ahead of them that they neglect their own plans.

The solution, if you or someone you know has this ailment, is to expand your perception of the world. See the abundance in everything around you from the fruits on the trees, to the vastness of the sky, to the depths of your soul. Develop an abundance mentality that states there is more than anyone can consume in this world. There is enough business for three more companies to enter your market. When you radiate that philosophy, you will begin to attract that abundance in your life. In order to live out the true meaning of the tenet, you must live unselfishly. You should give freely of yourself and share your fruits with others who are less fortunate.

A poem by Robert Collier captures the essence of this thought:

We must share
If we keep the blessing from above
Failing to share we fail to have
Such is the law of love

Fundamentally, you should be a person who rejoices in

human triumph. You will become outer directed and objective in your thinking. Such an attitude brings more back to you than all your selfish efforts could possibly produce. In the last days of existence, you will find that everything you will receive will be all the things you gave away. In serving others, the first priority should be to solve a problem or meet a need for someone else. It should not be to gain something from others. This attitude brings more back to you, and the life cycle begins again. Selflessness is not the objective; rather, graciousness is the key in all your human dealings. When we encourage others, they will encourage us. Each of us benefits when one experiences success. Other's prosperity is circulated throughout the community, which creates jobs for others, which strengthens the entire society. It is important to be a fan of others, and you will find that you will be the beneficiary.

Questions for Empowerment

1. Do you have an abundance mentality?

2. How do you circulate prosperity?

3. Who are some of your mentors?

4. Who are you mentoring to?

5. What drives you to excel?

Scroll VII

To Be Just as Enthusiastic about the Success of Others as You Are about Your Own

I entered into this world alone and dependent, and I shall also make my exit alone. The space between these two periods is called life. It is my objective to fill these moments with people. I will develop a love for all people. I shall reach out to all people, and seek out those individuals who are faster, slower, whiter, darker, taller, shorter, smarter, more challenged, richer, and poorer. I will respect all people and will concentrate on their commonalties instead of their differences. I will look for the good in everyone and in doing so I will reveal the best that is in me. I will learn to accept others on their terms and not my own terms. I will learn to listen attentively and not just hear words. Rather, I will focus on the meaning and feelings behind their words, which will make all my communication better. I will strive to comprehend before I attempt to persuade others. I believe that all men and women are my brothers and sisters. I will work on creating interdependence with others to ensure their success and my own. I will encourage and inspire others to reach their full potential, and in doing so I will tap into my own inherent potential. I will be dependable and reliable to others. I will give of myself unselfishly to others. As it is written, there is no greater love than to lay down one's life for his brother. I will put service over self-interest and will reap my harvest.

Tenet VII

To forget the mistakes of the past and press on to greater achievements of the future

The past has an unwarranted power over the lives of most people. All the past exists entirely in memory, yet it has the amazing ability to continue to control and manipulate the present moment. Think about that for a moment. The past, this invisible non-entity, continues to wreck the lives of millions of people every day. The past with no physical shape can wrestle your life away from you if you allow it. To improve the quality of your life, it is essential to follow the next tenet, which states, "To forget the mistakes of the past, and press on to the greater achievements of the future."

Ralph Waldo Triner wrote an interesting book entitled *The Greatest Thing Ever Known*. In it he captures the essence of the tenet. "He has no regrets for the past because before he entered into his present consciousness, he was in a sense unto life and all regrets that he might have for the past are now swallowed up in the joy that the new birth that has brought fullness of life continually spreads before his every step". He continues, "Peace, a full abiding peace, is continually his." It can be yours as well if you learn to live out the meaning of this powerful life-changing tenet.

The only redeeming characteristic of the past is the life lessons that are branded into your memory. The past should be reviewed, analyzed, then discarded, but it should not be traded in for one second of the present moment. As I stated, the secret of an optimistic and peaceful life is first of all to live in the present moment. It seems that man is obsessed with the past and future and misses out on the very essence of life, which is this very moment.

A poet wrote,

As I picked up the old tool
Envisioning my new creation's end
Amassing all my many years of school
Drawing together the then, now and when
Uniting the basic elements that incites life to begin

You can develop and learn from the past, you can plan and envision the future, but the moment cannot be saved, but must be lived immediately. The second part of an optimistic life is to learn to forgive. The load of negative emotion caused by not forgiving others can extract a tremendous amount of life energy as you continue to haul this unwanted cargo. First of all, you need to forgive yourself for allowing yourself to be in a position that made you vulnerable.

Secondly, forgive the people who may wrong you. You continue to allow others to control your emotions when you don't forgive them. Forgiveness releases the attachment to the offending event and frees up much needed life energy to distribute to other activities.

As we bury our past, we begin to build our future. According to Mr. Larson,

"The man who finds it easier to forgive than to condemn is on the verge of superior wisdom and higher spiritual power. He has entered the path to real greatness, and may rapidly rise in the scale by applying the laws of true human development. Instead of producing weakness and indifference, the act of absolute forgiveness will produce a more powerful character, a more brilliant mind and a greater soul."

Are there times when it is not acceptable to forgive others? Forgiveness is a remedy to our own problems. It takes place in the heart of our emotions. It is not intended to benefit our oppressors; rather it is to free ourselves from the events which imprison us.

Memory can recreate events with such clarity as to trigger our nervous system to respond as if the events were happening in the present moment. It seems that the greater the intensity of feeling during the event the more vivid it is to remember. When someone continually focuses on the event, they implant the images in their mind.

As one relives the event, they keep the negative event

alive in their mind, which causes them to assimilate all the emotions concerning the event.

The key is to disregard the natural tendency to think about what happened. Train your mind to replace the thought with something positive. It is critical to understand that we all must fail to finally win. The truth is that no one fails until one quits. My coach always told us players that winners never quit, and quitters never win. In order to win in the game of life, you must learn from your mistakes and the temporary setbacks, and then forget them. The secret to this mode of thinking is that failure is not possible because everything you do produces a result. That result allows you to learn in order to improve the performance for the next time. The experience is always a positive one because you were you able to grow emotionally, mentally and professionally from the event. If all you do is to dwell only on past perceived failed events; then those events can only serve as imaginary roadblocks in your life.

The wisdom of Victor Hugo reminds us,

"To live, is to understand. To live is to smile at the present, to look toward posterity over the wall. To live is to have in one's self a balance, and to weigh in it the good and the evil. To live is to have justice, truth, reason, devotion, probity, sincerity, commonsense, right, and duty nailed to the heart."

In order to press on to greater achievements of the

future, you must know what you want your future to look like. In the words of Mr. Larson, "Know what you desire to become; resolve to become what you desire to become." Commit yourself to forgetting the mistakes from your past and press on to greater achievements for your future.

As the scriptures teach in Philippians 3:13-14, "Forgetting what is behind and straining toward what is ahead, I press on toward the goal to win the prize for which God has called me heavenward in Christ Jesus." Always move in the direction of your dreams and leave the past in the shadows.

Questions for Empowerment

1. How often do you dwell on past failures?

2. Name the valuable lesson that you learned from your temporary set back.

3. What steps did you take to correct the situation?

4. Who in your life is unforgiven?

5. Can you visualize the future that you desire?

Scroll VIII

To Forget the Mistakes of the Past and Press on to Greater Achievements for the Future

As an old song's lyric rings, "I will try to remember to forget." This is my secret for happy living. In order for me to enjoy my life fully, I must have all my faculties immersed in the present moment of time. I now know that life is this next breath that I take, it is acting out the plans that I make. Life is an ever-moving dynamic force that carries willing participants to their dreams. It is wisdom that teaches me that in order to build my future, I must bury my past no matter how pleasant or displeasing it has been. The past is the weakest form of energy. It has no ability to step into the present or the future to alter it. The past exists entirely in memory that will quickly fade away until it is turned into dust that is blown into the far northern winds. Nature doesn't think of its past events; rather it uses all its power to complete its daily mission. Its total focus is on raising the new day and welcoming in the night. It does not have the time to think of days passed, nor should I. It nurtures the earth as a mother her young. So too will I nurture my life with no regard for yesterday, but only for the next breath and my next step. I will sensitize myself to understand fully what it means to be alive. I will look on all things with a new focus and embrace this priceless gift of life that has been given to me free and clear. I will exercise my free will to make the right decisions, which will lead to the right direction for my life. The dimension of time—past, present, and future—cannot exist together in my thoughts, so I choose to fill this thought in the now. From this day forward, I will live this day as it was meant, which is fully lived in the moment.

James Rankin

Tenet VIII

**To wear a cheerful countenance, and give
every living creature you meet a smile**

The next tenet reminds us to wear a cheerful countenance, and give every living creature we meet a smile. Webster's Dictionary defines countenance as, "the expression on a face, approval, favor, to condone." In order to follow this tenet, you need to wear a sincere smile, which reflects the love in your heart.

To smile reflects a love for your fellow-man. In fact, to love your fellow-man is our greatest commandment, and our greatest challenge. When we live with the philosophy that we will wear a cheerful countenance and give every living creature a smile we must immerse ourselves in love. In order to understand true love we must study where it first originated. I Corinthians 13:4-8 you will find one of the best definitions of love ever written,

> "Love is patient, love is kind. It does not envy, it does not boast, it is not proud. It is not rude, it is not self-seeking, it is not easily angered, it keeps no record of wrongs. Love does not delight in evil but rejoices

with the truth. It always protects, always trusts, always hopes, always perseveres. Love never fails."

It is true love when you can sincerely get more pleasure giving than receiving. One of the greatest traits an Optimist can possess is a sincere love for all of mankind.

On the subject of love for our fellow-man, Og Mandino wrote in his best seller *The Greatest Salesman in the World,*

"I will love the ambitious for they can inspire me. I will love the failures for they can teach me. I will love the kings for they are but human; I will love the meek for they are divine. I will love the rich for they are yet lonely; I will love the poor for they are so many; I will love the young for the faith they hold; I will love the old for the wisdom they share. I will love the beautiful for their eyes of sadness; I will love the ugly for their souls of peace."

It has been said that the secret to our existence is to love what we do for a profession, and to develop a deep meaningful love for the people we serve. Give with a glad heart, or don't give at all. Being cheerful reflects this philosophy. Christian Larson writes about cheerfulness: "To attain the cheerful state we must remember that it is a product of the inner life and does not come from circumstances or conditions; therefore, the first essential is to create a cheerful world in the imagination; picture in your mind the brightest states of existence that you can think of and impress joy upon the mind at all times; feel joy, think joy, and make every action of mind and body thrill with joy; ere long you will have created within yourself, and the subconscious will be the cause of joy, and when this is done, cheerfulness and brightness will become permanent elements in yourself."

You might think that is going overboard. It is pure fantasy to expect individuals to live their lives in a state of euphoria. Yet, it is the belief that you can live in a positive state of mind and positively impact the lives of others that gives rise to the possibility that it can and will occur.

Such focus is the recognition that all of life is important and vibrates with energy, that everything and everyone has a purpose and talent that can be shared with the world. With that purpose and talent, everyone has a responsibility to develop himself or herself and share their gifts with others. It is our responsibility to light up a room, become a shoulder for someone in need, and be a mentor for others. Cheerfulness will become a reality for you when you begin to live out the meaning of the creed.

The second part of the tenet teaches us to respect all living things regardless of how insignificant you might think something might be. Yes, I have been known to escort a moth or a cricket out of a room and into the freshness of nature. Extreme, you may say. I don't think so because there is living intelligence present in all things.

When you respect life, nature will reciprocate to you. I am reminded of a poem of William Blake that states,

Little Fly
Thy summer play
My thoughtless hand
Has brushed away
Are thou
A man like me?
Or am I
A fly like thee?

This simple poem reminds us that although we have been given domain over all the creatures, we should respect and value all living things. Love is your armor and your tool that makes living this tenet of the creed truly effortless. In the words of Mr. Larson, "It is love that determines what we are to think, what we work for, where we are to go, and what we are to accomplish. Therefore among all the great essentials, the principal one is to know how to love." I have learned that you can discover a person's true nature by how they treatothers who cannot benefit them.

In fact, love is the solution to many of the world's woes. As we discussed earlier, when you love yourself you will act in a different manner than if you don't. This includes changing what you eat and drink, and how you speak to yourself. Secondly, when you have sincere love for your fellow-man, following the moral commandments becomes relatively easy. When you love, you don't kill, lie, covet, steal and dishonor others.

Questions for Empowerment

1. Do you value all living things?

2. Are you open to different views other than your own?

3. Have you read a book about a different religious, national or political subject other than your own?

4. When was the last time you smiled BIG?

5. Do you value yourself? What have you done recently that would illustrate it?

Scroll IX

To Wear a Cheerful Countenance and
Give Every Living Creature a Smile

All of my thoughts are transparent to others without a single word spoken. My mannerisms are the chosen token to communicate to the world how I feel. My habitual thoughts wear grooves into my face and can affect my heart's pace into either a slow calm rhythm or a raging inferno. This constant thought process is my countenance, which I carry with me every day of my life. Science teaches me that for every action there is an equal and opposite reaction. There is no greater trait that ensures quality living than a good positive countenance. My countenance acts as a highly charged magnetic field that attracts my thoughts back to me. If I desire good results in my life, then it can be traced to my current countenance's contents. The natural by-product of a healthy countenance is a big sincere smile. From this day forward I will wear this powerful expression and it will create magic in my life and the lives of others. My smile will lighten my load and shorten a long and tiring road. It will energize me as with my sincere smile I acknowledge the priming life energy from every living creature in the world. I will share my smile with all people for recognition of others is justified because everyone was created in the image of my creator. There is no greater expression that I have at my disposal than my smile. It can pick up one's spirit. Its unique quality requires of me to give it away to have it return rewards to me. My smile translates into all languages and creates a universal sign of happy, caring individuals that connects to the world.

James Rankin

Tenet IX

**To give so much time to the improvement of
yourself that you have no time to criticize others**

The biggest project you will ever work on is yourself. It
is truly the ultimate "do it yourself" project. The next tenet
says to give so much time to the improvement of yourself
that you have no time to criticize others.

The good news for you is that you are not subject to a
life sentence with you. You have the wonderful opportunity
and responsibility to improve any element in your life. The
famous psychiatrist Abraham Maslow wrote, "We have,
all of us, an impulse to improve ourselves, an impulse toward actualizing more of our potentialities toward human
fulfillment."

You are merely thoughts and by changing those thoughts
you will inevitably change yourself. When you witness
the change in yourself, you will begin to feel empowered.
Furthermore, in the development of yourself it is critical to
understand that if you maintain the same thought pattern
day in and day out, you will remain the same. As the old ranch
hand used to tell me, "If we continue to do what we have
always done, then we will always get what we have always
got." Mr. Larson teaches us that "continuous advancement

is the purpose of life; therefore, to live the right life is to live that life that promotes progress and growth, development and advancement in everything that pertains to life."

How can you improve yourself? What areas can you change? As in all development, progress begins with a question, and an honest assessment of yourself. A few of my favorite questions are "Are you where you planned to be last year? Are you happy with your development in financial, family, mental, social, and spiritual aspects of your life?" If not, it is time to get to work. The Optimist Creed can assist you by targeting important parts of your life and weaving them into a strong and stable foundation, on which to build your life. Christian Larson writes, "Make yourself over, so to speak, in your own friendship; increase your personal worth; polish your own character, refine your mind; and make real, and more of the ideal; double and triple your love and your kindness and constantly increase your admiration for everything that has real quality and high worth."

There are many successful people who, because of their circumstances and background, have had to recreate themselves. It has been said that children take on the self-esteem of their parents unless they consciously make an effort to change. You can reprogram yourself to become the person you strive to be.

Mr. Larson says, "The average person fails to improve because he lives mainly in the consciousness of his imperfections; he feels that he is ordinary and constantly impresses the subconscious with the feeling of the ordinary; the subconscious naturally responds by producing the ordinary, both in mind and body."

It is your responsibility to take charge of the thoughts that enter your mind. To focus constantly on the possibility of growth is the key to improvement. One very effective way to aid in this endeavor is to use affirmations. An affirmation is a form of self-talk that assists in the reprogramming of your subconscious mind. Some of my affirmations are:

- Each day I am developing into a better, smarter and more loving person.

- I like myself because I always take constructive action to make things happen.

- I strive to be perfect because I never make mistakes knowingly.

- I am happy because I choose to be happy.

- God is beautiful, nature is beautiful, and I am beautiful.

Another important affirmation comes from Mr. Larson,

"Think of yourself as gaining ground along all lines, as finding better and better circumstances, as increasing in power and ability, and becoming more healthful in body, more vigorous and brilliant in mind, more perfect in character, and more powerful in soul."

However, the best affirmations can be found in the Optimist Creed written by Christian Larson. In order to be effective, affirmations must not be superficially recited. The words must seep deep into your sub-conscious mind, that mind that never sleeps and forms the images which determine your dreams. Mr. Larson remarks,

> "It is therefore evident that when we cease to live on the surface of personal life; we shall constantly improve that surface; by mentally living in the within we shall strengthen, enrich and perfect the without; that is; we improve external effect by going more deeply into the subconscious and increasing the quality and the power of internal causes."

Your thoughts affect every aspect of your life including your dream world. The Indians used to believe that a man had two lives, his physical life and his dream world.

In order to reach the pinnacle of our dreams, we must learn to connect to the great power within ourselves. The best example that illustrates this mode of thought is the iceberg. The part of the ice that is protruding from the water's surface represents your conscious mind. However, the massive part of the iceberg is not visible to the eye but is just below the surface. That is the way it is with your sub-conscious mind. The sub-conscious is that part of you that regulates everything you do, and your results can be traced to that vast area of your inner self that has rarely been explored. When you begin to chart the "New World" you will find great treasures.

Mr. Larson taught that everyone has the potential to tap into the riches located in the great within, which give us all the opportunity to remake ourselves in the exact likeness of all that is great and beautiful and ideal.

Mr. Larson explained,

"Every upward step that is taken in mind adds power to the mind, and this added power will produce added results in the tangible world. When these added results are observed, then mind gain more faith in itself and more faith always brings more power."

It should be a natural course for man to live his life with the understanding that there is unlimited potential in himself, and that he should continue to grow in every area of his life.

The fundamental element for improvement is having the confidence in yourself, and the belief that you can improve in every area of your life. This is all possible by the presence of belief reinforced with faith.

Faith is the key, which opens up your consciousness to the notion that the impossible is possible. There are solutions to every problem you have. Faith is the starting point of all self-improvement. Mr. Larson teaches us that,

"As we grow in faith, the finer creative energies increase in power, because the more faith we have, the more power we receive from within; we thereby promote the development of talent, genius and rare ability on an ever-increasing scale."

As we have discussed earlier, you are the sum total of all the past thinking you have done, and what you become in the future will be based on what you are thinking right now. Think about that for a moment. Energize all your thoughts with the strength of faith. An impediment to our growth is that we can become easily bored with the very things that will assist us in our development.

If you were to examine why we lose interest, you will find that you have fulfilled your natural curiosity concerning the object of your attention.

If you want to regain that newness in whatever it is that you have suddenly become bored with, rekindle your initial attraction to the hobby, job, or that special someone in your life. Never stop asking questions and searching for answers concerning it. Once you have developed a reservoir of information, you will have attained a working knowledge of your subject matter. The more you grow in your subject matter, the more conviction you will have about it. As your conviction is fortified, your passion will swell within you.

When you contact all the points expressed in this passage you will discover the truth. When you learn your subject, the more knowledge you will obtain. The more knowledge you obtain, the more conviction you will radiate. The more conviction you radiate, the more passion you will possess. This formula will create a zest for life that will ensure that you never experience a dull moment on your journey in life. Too many people pass through life without living in the present moment. Too many times we trade today's joy for the miseries of the past or for a promise in the future. The truly happy optimistic people have realized that success really is a journey and not a destination.

A poet wrote,

The dream finally in my grasp
After all the times of trying
I thought the euphoria would last
However, fond were the years of striving
The true joy was the journey past

Questions for Empowerment

1. How much time do you spend on the improvement of yourself?

2. What new things have you learned this month?

3. Have you formulated your personal affirmations?

4. Have you committed the creed to memory?

5. Are you enjoying your journey to your goals?

Scroll X

To Give So Much Time to the Improvement of Yourself that You Have No Time to Criticize Others

I am like a block of marble. Deep inside the block is the beauty of a sculpture. However, it is hidden from the untrained eye. Inside everyone is a bigger, smarter, and better person waiting to make its entrance. The initial step to accomplish this objective is through careful evaluation and introspection. Just as the artist can form art with a chisel, so too can I chip away the negative elements in my body, mind, and spirit. I know that what is weak can be made strong, what is dark and can be made light, and what is wrong can be made right. The Master Optimist Larson reminds me that with my belief in the notion of self-improvement I can give my body added strength, give my mind added brilliancy, and give my soul added inspiration. Every day I choose the path of self-improvement and refinement. I believe that every day of my life I can make advancement in every area of my life. I will emphasize every area of my life for I know that I am a multidimensional person. The only path to be fully developed is to concentrate of all areas of my life, which is comprised of my professional, physical, mental, financial, personal, and spiritual elements. The only way to ensure that this wisdom is applied in my life is to utilize the momentum of motivation found in the seeds of a single goal. I will learn to set goals in each of these areas. The fruits from my labor will not rule me. Rather, I will maintain the proper attitude concerning materialism. The truth always reveals that man is not what he has, but what he is. I will constantly and consistently smooth out the rough edges of my individuality every day. It only takes one more degree of heat to turn water into steam, and just an additional single swing of an ax can bring down the tallest and thickest tree. So too does it take one more attempt to accomplish my objective whatever it may be, and to become the person I have designed for myself. For I know that my initial creation is in my mind, and that is then formed into my words. Those powerful centered words are reinforced through my constructive preplanned action and my belief and expectancy this picture until one day I will have reached the treasure buried deep inside of me.

James Rankin

Tenet X

To be too large for worry, too noble for anger, too strong for fear, and too happy to permit the presence of trouble

The last tenet is perhaps one of the most challenging of all the tenets. It states that we should be too large for worry, too noble for anger, too strong for fear, and too happy to permit the presence of trouble. How would your life be different if you were to eliminate worry, anger, and fear from it? It can be compared to the sunrise, which breaks through from the early morning fog. There would be a new more brilliant focus to your life. You would experience an almost weightless existence. Let's examine this tenet to discover its hidden truth. Did you know worry's siblings are doubt and uncertainty?

The great philosopher Fichte captures a possible remedy when he wrote,

"The religious man is forever secured from the possibility of doubt and uncertainty. In every moment he knows distinctly what he wills; for the innermost root of life—his will—forever flows forth from the Divinity, immediately and without the possibility of error; its indication is infallible, and for that indication he has an infallible perception. In every moment he knows that in all Eternity he shall know what he shall will, and ought to will; that in all Eternity the fountain of Divine Love which has burst forth in him shall never be dried up, but shall uphold him securely and bear him on forever."

It is our nature to live without worry. Worry should not be allowed to occupy your mind. The presence of worry is something you pick up from your environment. It is sometimes fueled by an overzealous media, which seems to thrive on controversies, tragedies, and downturns in our economy.

It has been said that early in a child's development he learns more from what is caught from his parents than what he is taught.

The apostle Paul teaches us in Philippians 4:6-8,

"Do not be anxious about anything, but in everything, by prayer and petition, with thanksgiving, present your requests to God. And the peace of God, which transcends all understanding, will guard your hearts and your minds in Christ Jesus. Finally, brothers, whatever is true, whatever is noble, whatever is right, whatever is pure, whatever is lovely, whatever is admirable—if anything is excellent or praiseworthy—think about such things."

This tenet will provide you a protective shield against

the arrows of the world's pessimism, which leads us to doubt our abilities. When doubt enters your conscious state, dismiss it immediately with your overwhelming faith. Fear is your ego's voice defying your personal growth. When you ignore the whisper, and focus on the end result, you will find your victory.

This victory is possible when you equip yourself with the strength of words. In the beginning that is all there was, and the same truth is evident in your life. It all starts with your words. One word, if allowed to permeate throughout your life will assist you in honoring the last tenet. That word is Faith. Faith can transform anyone's life in a very real and meaningful way. Faith is a word that has made all things a reality. It was the spark that propelled human beings into the belief that they could accomplish something for themselves and for society. An optimist's positive attitude is built on the foundation of faith. An optimist truly sees the possible in the impossible, the solution in the problem, the joy in the pain.

The scriptures teach us that faith is the things hoped for. Mr. Larson expounds on this when he writes, "Faith is the evidence of things not seen, because faith does see what has not been seen; faith knows that the unseen is real and substantial; faith proves that the unseen can be seen by those who will awaken the superior mind within; therefore, by entering into faith we enter into the realization of the real and see all things as they are in the perfect state." The perfect state is the fulfillment of the tenets of the Optimist Creed on a daily basis.

As we begin to analyze the last tenet, we find the first part points out that we should be too large for worry. My grandfather taught me that worry is like a rocking chair in that it gives you something to do with your time, but it never gets you anywhere. Worry can exist only where there is no deep-rooted faith. Worry is a state of anticipated fear of failure. Mr. Larson teaches us that,

> "While in faith the mind has no fear of failure; faith sees the possibilities of success; faith knows that success in every instance is possible because it knows that all things are possible; faith does not ask if success will come, but opens the mind to the great power within that positively will produce success."

In life, ninety percent of results are founded not in an event itself, but rather how you respond to it. There are solutions to every problem. Moreover, we have to fail so many times finally to reach our expected goal. Once I met a young man who sold cars for a living. In only his second year he sold more than four hundred cars. That is quite an amazing record. However, he told me about his other record, which seemed to give just as much satisfaction. The record was the longest time frame without selling a car in his dealership. This would have been a time when most people would have quit.

Success is just within arm's reach when most individuals throw in the towel. Sports stars provide some great examples for us. Let's name just a few. Babe Ruth held the record for the most homeruns in Major League Baseball for many years and he also held the record for the most strikeouts. Wilt Chamberlain holds the records for scoring the most points in a National Basketball Association game, and he also holds the record for missing the most free throws in a game.

In a recent conversation, Hall of Famer St. Louis Cardinal Lou Brock mentioned that the first time at bat in the Big Leagues, the first three pitches were strikes, yet he went on to become a great ball player. In American politics everyone is familiar with the failures of Abraham Lincoln, which included losing two elections and failing in business. However, he went on to become one of our greatest presidents. It was President Lincoln's character, passion, and determination that held our nation together during the Civil War.

The wisdom instilled in these examples is that failure is an intrinsic part of success. Failure is the part of the journey that molds our character, strengthens our inner spirit, and prepares us for our success. Every successful person who has overcome failure has had a success-focused attitude. Your attitude is the condition you work in during your journey through life. A good positive attitude can be likened to a magnet. It will attract to you that which you seek. Earl

Nightingale has defined attitude as a position or bearing indicating action, feeling and moods. It is your actions, feelings and moods that inevitably determine your success or failure in life.

Chuck Swindoll describes attitude in this way,

> "The longer I live, the more I realize the impact of attitude in life. Attitude, to me, is more important than fact, it is more important than the past, than education, than money, than circumstances, than failure, than success, than what other people think or say or do. It is more important than appearance, giftedness or skill. It will make or break a company, a church, a home. The remarkable thing is we have a choice every day regarding the attitude we will embrace for that day. We cannot change our past ... we cannot change the fact that people will act in a certain way. We cannot change the inevitable. The only thing we can do is play on the one string we have, and that is our attitude."

Attitude can be scaled down to one's habitual train of thought. Positive thoughts on a continual basis will produce a positive attitude. Furthermore, it is your attitude in the temporary times of failure that will determine when you are back in the victory column.

The next part of the tenet states that you should be too noble for anger. Anger is a very destructive trait that prevents individuals from reaching their full potential. It can be likened to a cancerous cell in the body. The body may continue functioning; however, sooner than later the effects will begin to surface wreaking all types of havoc.

Anger ruins relationships and can rob you of two of the most precious gifts a human being possess—peace and tranquility. A body and mind at peace are more productive than those in turmoil.

It has been said that you can learn more about an individual in a time of crisis, than you can in years of prosperity. You can also learn about an individual by measuring the things that can set them off. What is it that sets you oft? Anger is a part of life; however, it is important to learn how to handle anger when it surfaces. Anger must be funneled into specific outlets to defuse it and transform it into a useable, more productive emotion.

You need to identify your anger, and address it immediately. Anger is not something you want to bottle up inside you. Have the kind of relationships with friends and family that allow you to talk out your anger, and then proceed to invent options to overcome the situation which produced the anger. Then execute constructive actions to change the situation. Next, put a strategy into action which will prevent the situation from happening again.

A trait that all true optimists possess is self-control. The ability to control one's emotions and actions separates us from the animals. Human beings no longer have to rely solely on their instincts; rather all human beings should live by their intuition.

The next part of the tenet states that we should be too strong for fear. Fear is present on many different levels in humans. There is the fear of failure, fear of success, fear of heights, fear of falling. Fear is a part of every human being unless it is recognized and resolved. When you live in faith, you will discover that overcoming these fears will be relatively easy.

The lack of faith is the root of many of the inherent fears we all experience. You must conquer fear by facing reality head on. According to Mr. Larson,

> "To banish fear, have faith; the only infallible remedy for fear is faith; faith in all things, and at all times. Faith sees the substance and gains the substance; fear sees the shadow and is soon left with nothing but the shadow."

It is that attitude that paves the thought that you can succeed in anything you desire in life. It is critical that you free your mind of negative attitudes and beliefs and stimulate your imagination with thoughts that are positive. Live your life day by day with the strength of principle and truth. President Franklin D. Roosevelt, in one of the most distressing times in our modern history, captured a powerful thought about fear in his 1936 inaugural speech when he said, "The only thing we have to fear is fear itself the nameless, meaningless thing that paralyzes needed efforts that converts retreat into action."

Face your fear head on and eliminate its stronghold on your life. The only way to defeat fear in its track is to clothe yourself in the garment of faith. Fortify yourself with the truth that Mr. Larson has so brilliantly written and captured in the tenets of the creed.

He continues his discussion on faith,

> "The more we depend upon this power the more of this power we shall receive, until our capacity becomes enormous. The more we exercise faith, the more faith we shall secure; and the more faith we have in faith the more deeply we shall enter into the very soul of faith."

Faith is essential to peace of mind. It is not that we must live without fear; rather we should learn to deal with the inherent fears that are present in our life. It is only when the fear paralyzes us from growth that it becomes a serious problem. Courage is not the absence of fear in life; rather, it is your willingness to march forward in spite of fear.

I do realize that not all fear is imaginary. During the writing for this book our nation was attacked by terrorists. In an almost surreal scene these terrorists hijacked four commercial airplanes and used two of them as missiles to destroy the twin towers of the World Trade Center in New York City. Another hijacked plane crashed into the

Pentagon in Arlington, Virginia. It was reported that brave passengers on a flight leaving Pittsburgh overpowered the hijackers on the plane, which would have been used to destroy a target in Washington D.C. Unfortunately, the plane crashed in a deserted area, killing all people aboard.

Thousands of citizens lost their lives in these tragic events, and thousand more were injured in the worst attack on American soil since December 7, 1941 when Japan attacked Pearl Harbor. Initially, fear gripped our nation. However President George W. Bush, in decisive leadership, grounded every commercial and private plane in United States air space. That has never happened in aviation history. This constructive action very well could have saved thousands of additional lives, and foiled other terrorists' schemes. Our financial markets were closed for four days. The last time our markets were closed for that long was in 1918 during World War I. Despite all of this, the American people stood strong and united to assist in this bleak period in our history. Hundred of volunteers assisted in locating people from the tons of rubble. People gave clothes, money, and contributed millions of pints of blood for the victims. Our people were too strong for fear. Calling these actions an "act of war," President Bush with unshakeable confidence proclaimed, "Make no mistake: The United States will hunt down those responsible for these cowardly acts." He went on to say, "Freedom and fear are at war." Think about that next time you are face to face with your fear. Are you going to let this invisible emotion dictate what you do in life?

It is important that you believe you can overcome your fears whatever they may be. Hans O. Gerz, MD writes on the treatment of phobic and obsessive-compulsive behavior. He teaches us a valuable strategy for overcoming our fears, which utilizes Victor Frankl's paradoxical intention. The paradoxical intention allows you to face your fear head-on with amazing results. Dr. Gerz writes,

> "A characteristic phenomenon in the phobic neurosis is anticipatory anxiety the fear of various symptoms such as passing out, blushing, becoming panicky when riding in cars, buses, crossing bridges; the fear of heights, heart palpitation, etc. Such anticipatory anxiety frequently will cause the symptoms to actually materialize. The more the patient fears the occurrence of the symptom and the more he tries to avoid it, the more liable it is to occur."

Paradoxical intention is the classical example of the self-fulfilling prophecy. It is the acting out of that which you fear. If you fear that you will mentally go blank when you are speaking to someone, then prepare to go blank. Face your fear boldly, and you will conquer it. Dr. Gerz continues, "The removal of the fear will strangle the neurotic symptoms; subsequently the patient will find out that, paradoxically, the more he tries to produce his symptoms, the more he finds himself completely unable to do so."

Don't let fear dictate what you do in life. Instead, ignore it and push forward to growth and prosperity. Mr. Larson writes,

> "Fear is a feeling that feels the coming of ills or other things we do not want; and as we always express through our words the feeling that we fear, we form tendencies toward those things, and the creative powers within us will produce them."

Always focus in on what you want and use your thoughts and actions to obtain it.

As I mention throughout this book, your thoughts are magnetic in nature, and will attract to you whatever it is that you think. It doesn't matter if it is good or bad, beautiful or ugly, uplifting or degrading. As surely as the moon will shine down on you tonight, you will materialize in your life your most dominant and persistent thoughts. Tell yourself that you will be too strong for fear. Then begin to visualize what strength looks like to you.

Mr. Larson writes,

> "To think of truth we can never admit that we are weak: we cannot even admit that it is possible for us to become weak. When we feel weak, we are simply permitting ourselves to be untrue to ourselves; we ignore the reality of our own being and cause the mind to create conditions in our system that are false."

Thus evil begins. But so long as we cause the mind to be fixed in that great truth that God is our strength, we shall not be conscious of anything that is not strength; nor will the mind create any condition that is not true to the truth." The last part of the tenet states to be too happy to permit the presence of trouble. As I have previously mentioned in tenet two, happiness is a conscious decision that you make every day of your life. You are solely responsible for your happiness. Remember no one can take away your happiness because you are this happiness. It is an intricate part of who you are.

Is it within the realm of possibility to be too large for worry? Can you be too noble to allow anger to overtake your emotions? Can you be too strong for fear? Will you allow happiness to overshadow the presence of trouble? You control more than you ever imagined as it pertains to your life. Your inner world that you create gives rise to your outer world. You have a magnetic power, which draws to you that which you desire consciously or unconsciously. Are you aware of what you are attracting into your life? If not, you now have the necessary information to make that change.

Despite what some people want you to believe, change takes place instantaneously. The change begins in your mind with your reasoning capabilities. It then flows into your heart, the home of your emotions. It proceeds into the iron of your will to become a permanent part of your makeup.

The underlying question should be: How would being more optimistic change your life? First, incorporating optimism will change the lenses through which you view your world. You will look for the best in every situation. Adopting this optimistic philosophy will lighten your load as you journey through this life. Being optimistic, you will be able to disregard all your preconceived, preconditioned responses to life. You will face the world boldly, courageously and expectantly. You will become more magnetic drawing everything to you that you need to reach every desire of your heart. The desire that you produce in your heart wants to experience fulfillment. With an optimistic attitude you will respond in kind with the necessary action.

Next, you will experience the euphoric feeling of accomplishment. You will feel the joy of seeing the physical manifestation of an invisible nerve impulse produced in your brain. You transform your thoughts into reality and see how your thoughts and ideas have positively impacted the lives of others.

Embracing these ten dynamic tenets will harness deep inside you your untapped potential. When you become an optimistic person you will unleash that part of yourself that your ego has tied down. The ego has grounded too many people in a routine, predictable and mediocre existence. Optimism will burn out the negativity, doubts and worry that plague our society.

When you are optimistic you will be launched into a new

consciousness, new heights and new results. Your transformation cannot be measured in numbers, but only through the lives you touch. There will come a day when the sun has completed its course across the sky with its brilliant colors stretched out in every direction.

You will look down upon the earth and see happy, productive, and prosperous optimists as far as the eye can see. As you glide across the boundless sky, you will know that you contributed to its present state, and the feeling will warm you as you begin your next segment of your eternal journey. We have covered a lot of territory as we have studied the creed. The purpose of this little book was to create an awareness of the power of the Optimist Creed. Next time you read the Optimist Creed, you will be reminded of this time we have spent together.

The words of T.S. Elliot captured the essence of this thought when he wrote, "We will never cease our striving, yet when the striving is over, we would have arrived where we first began, but we will know it for the first time."

Many readers have recited this creed for years, and have never internalized the power of the words. You will be amazed when you read the Optimist Creed again after studying the *Power of the Creed* just what a gem Mr. Larson has created to assist you.

Although we live in an unpredictable, unstable and sometimes scary world, the one thing that you can count on is by adopting optimism as a way of life you will have available to you a predictable and reliable philosophy which will stabilize your life. The cornerstones for your life should be peace, joy, reason and unyielding optimism. The Optimist Creed, when embodied by you, will create a persona that is too large for worry, too noble for anger and too happy to permit the presence of trouble. By incorporating the Optimist Creed into your life you will empower your own life in a dramatic and effective way.

Questions for Empowerment

1. What do you worry about?

2. How do you control your temper?

3. What do you fear in your life?

4. Do you experience true joy for living?

5. What steps can you take to eliminate those negative traits from your personality and embody joy in your life?

Recommended Reading

Of Dreams and Deeds by Gordon S. Thompson

Your Forces and How to Use Them by Christian Larson

The Ideal Made Real by Christian Larson

The Great Within by Christian Larson

The Greatest Salesman in the World by Og Mandino

The Greatest Thing Ever Known by Ralph Waldo Trine

Atlas Shrugged by Ayn Rand

Pulling Your Own Strings by Wayne Dyer

The Power of Positive Thinking by Norman V. Peale

How to Win Friends and Influence Others by Dale
    Carnegie

Riches Within by Robert Collier

Poems from the Spirit of Hope by J.M. Rankin

The Magic of Method Selling by J.M. Rankin

Living the Magic by J.M. Rankin

Nature by Ralph Waldo Emerson

Bible by the inspiration of the creator

Scroll XI

To be too Large for Worry, too Noble for Anger and too Happy to Permit the Presence of Trouble

As the eagle steps off the cliff and enters into the ecstasy of flight, so do I step into the direction of my dreams. Instilling the eagle's faith into my life bestows onto me new eyes to view my world.

With my new eyes I am able to see the unseen. I am able to bring into focus the physical manifestation of my desires, hopes and dreams. I will wear my faith as a second skin that will protect me from doubt, fear and worry. I will approach all my activities as though they were as I wish them to be. I understand that adopting faith in my life will empower me, which will give rise to that part of myself that can and will accomplish all that I want in my life. The amazing magical quality of faith is that the more I use it, the more faith that will be received into my life. I will approach all things with faith and I will witness a new birth in everything that comes into contact with me during my journey through this life.

Scroll XII
The Power of the Creed

These ten tenets will serve as lighthouses for my life. As the random storms appear on the horizon, I will not panic for now I hold the compass that keeps me on course. With the power of the Creed I see the light's glow, which allows me to navigate my way to my port of peace and serenity. Each tenet is fashioned with wisdom, and equips me to handle any of life's situations. The Creed strengthens my inner fortitude that protects my peace of mind. It will assist me in forming an alliance with my great within. I communicate to all living creatures my optimism. The creed educates me to nurture my friendships, and to give of myself to others. I choose to live the philosophy of optimism, which allows me to see the sunny side of everything. I expect the best from myself in everything that I am involved in my life. I rejoice in the successes of others, and take advantage of every opportunity to mentor to others. The creed reminds me to forget my past, and focus on the positive opportunities of the future. I show the world my optimism everyday with a big broad smile. I dedicate myself to life long learning that will improve my body, mind and spirit. I will have dominion over negative emotions, which secures my inner self from the arrows of the world. I have been recreated into a new person that radiates in the light of Optimism.

James Rankin

Lost Tenents of the Creed

Professor Brown wore a cap to hide his white bald head. The chemotherapy had begun, and he was trying to keep his schedule during the treatment. He met Paul in his classroom. The students were filing out when Paul stepped in. "Professor Brown, you wanted to see me."

"Yes Paul, I wanted to inform you of something that I think will help your project."

"I am all ears, sir."

"Well, it is interesting, but a friend of mine was invited to a civic club and received their creed," he said.

"It is an Optimist Club creed and it is written by Christian Larson. Yes, this could really help my project. Thank you, sir; you have been a real benefit."

Paul couldn't find any books at the library, so he went on the internet. He tried his luck on eBay and found an old book by Christian Larson written back in 1910. A week later, the small book arrived. Paul sat on his front porch as the wind kicked up the water's foam and as the white caps of the waves created an eye catching show. The wind gently combed through the palm trees in front of his condo. He was absorbed in the book, and went back into the house. He laid the book down, and lay on the sofa. He drifted off into a deep sleep.

After the fog cleared, Paul found himself in a park; he

saw a man in his thirties sitting on a park bench. He looked down to see a newspaper dated November 12, 1909. He knew that this man was Christian Larson. The man was reading a manuscript and was marking some of the text.

Paul walked up to the man. "Excuse me sir, may I sit with you? I see that you are reading a manuscript; is that yours?"

"Yes, it is. I think it is just about ready for publication. I wanted to have one more read in the tranquility of this lovely park in the silence of nature," Mr. Larson said.

"Sorry, sir, but there is a reason I am here now. I would like to hear about your book."

"You want to be a sounding board. That may not be a bad idea. You seem like a bright industrious young man. Let's see what you think about this," Mr. Larson said. "I have written twelve verses, and I feel very strongly that if anyone would follow their wisdom in their daily life they will have joy, pure joy."

"That is inspiring. That is what I have been seeking for my project. You have written the creed which can provide the insights into living an optimistic life. I am writing a piece on philosophy. So we do share a passion to help our fellow human beings live a better happier life," Paul said.

"You and I don't change anybody. In order for a person to change they must change their thought, because you are what you think; and to change your actions, you must change the purpose of your life, because every action is consciously or unconsciously inspired by the purpose held in view. To change their thought, one must be able to determine what impressions are to form in their mind, because every thought is created in the likeness of a mental impression," Mr. Larson stated.

"That is profound, sir. You tied in thought and purpose which represents action in one's life."

"Consequently, when one thinks what they desire to think, they will become what they desire to become. But to think what he desires to think, he must consciously govern the process through which impression are formed upon mind."

"How can that be done?" Paul asked.

"To govern this process is to have the power to exclude any impression from without that is not desired, and to completely impress upon mind every original thought that may be formed; thus giving mind the power to think only what it consciously chooses to think," Mr. Larson added.

"The theme is mastering self, isn't that right Mr. Larson?"

"Yes, self mastery is a prerequisite to a happy joyous life, but to value yourself correctly, understand the unbounded possibilities that are latent within you, and live in the realization of the greater things which you know you have the power to do. This will produce in mind the consciousness of superiority, and thoughts are his consciousness; superior impressions will be formed in the mind. From these impressions will come superior thoughts, which in turn will develop superiority in you, because a person is as he thinks," Mr. Larson said.

"Mr. Larson, what about people who were brought up in rough circumstances and don't have some of the advantages of others?"

"People need to begin their auto-emancipation by removing their attitude of self-submission. Cease to believe that you must remain down where you are. Change your mind; know that inherently you are master over everything in your own domain, and resolve to exercise your supremacy. Refuse to be impressed by your environment; and learn to impress your own mind with superior impressions only. Re-create your own mind according to a higher standard of power, ability and character; thus you will re-create both yourself and your surroundings; because by making yourself stronger and more competent, you will be wanted where surroundings are better, and recompense greater."

"What do we feed our mind, sir?" Paul asked.

"Anything that enters our mind while our mind is in the state of deep feeling, is deeply impressed; and it is the deepest impressions that serve as patterns for the creative energies. Love only that which has high worth, and never permit the common, the ordinary or the inferior to enter the world of feeling. Love the true side of life; love the soul side of a person; and love the greater possibilities that are latent in circumstances, conditions and things. Love these things with a passion that thrills every atom in your being. The result will be simply remarkable."

"When I find my purpose, I will discover my passion."

"Don't wait for your purpose, but count everything. Joy may at first seem difficult, but when we realize that the attitude of real joy rises above everything, and overcomes everything by taking life to a higher level, we shall soon find it easier and more natural to meet everything in joy than otherwise," Mr. Larson stated.

"That is it! It is temperament of existence. It is the Optimist philosophy. To continue in the consciousness of the law that underlies this idea will bring greater results and more rapid results, because in that case you will consciously direct the developing process, and you will know that to think you can, is to develop the power that you can."

"It is the power of positive thinking," Paul exclaimed.

"To keep constantly before mind, the idea that 'he can who thinks he can,' will steadily increases the qualities of faith, self-confidence, perseverance and persistence; and whoever develops these qualities to a greater and greater degree will move forward without fail. Therefore, to live in the conviction that 'he can who thinks he can,' will not only increase ability along with desired lines, but will also pro-duces the power to push that ability into a living, tangible action."

"In instructing people on the Philosophy of Optimism where do I begin?" Paul asked.

Mr. Larson walked to the window and looked out to view the bay. It was a deep blue and seemed to bubble with energy and life. "The human being is very much like the water. The truth is that the surface is beautiful as the sunlight reflects off its surface, but the real value lies beneath the surface. Human beings tend to live on the surface of life without digging into the vast unchartered regions of their minds."

"Yes, I agree with that. I am trying to figure out how to tap into the treasure," Paul replied.

"The initial stage for a person wanting to incorporate a new ideology in their life would have to be desire," Mr. Larson said.

"I have heard it said that desire is defined in a question which is, 'How much pain and suffering can you endure before you quit?' What do you think about that?"

"That is fine for a surface perspective. The purpose of desire is to inform man what he needs at every particular moment in order to supply the demands of change and growth in his life; and in promoting that purpose, desires give expression to its two leading functions. The first of these is to give the forces of the human system something definite to do and the second is to arouse those forces or faculties that have the natural power to do what is to be done."

"Desire provides direction in one's life," Paul stated.

"Yes, it is therefore evident that results in all lines of

endeavor depend very largely upon the power of desire, and that no one can afford to let his desires lag for a moment. The law should be: Know what you want, and then want it with all the life and power that is in you. Get your mind and your life fully aroused. Persistent desire will do this. And that it is most important to do; this is proven by the fact that in thousands of instances, a partly alive mind is the only reason why the goal in view has not been reached." Mr. Larson said.

"You have discovered the curse for unfulfilled dreams, Mr. Larson," Paul exclaimed.

"I want to emphasize, Paul, that the power of desire not only tends to arouse added life and power in these faculties upon which it may act, but it also tends to make the mind as a whole more alert and wide awake along those lines. This is well illustrated by the fact that when we have a strong, continuous desire for information on a certain subject, we always find someone or something that can give us that information. And the reason is that all the faculties of the mind are prompted by the force of his desire to be constantly on the look-out for that information. To make every desire subconscious, the subconscious mind should always be included in the process of desire; that is, whenever we express a desire we should think of the subconscious, and combine the thought of that desire without thought of the subconscious mind. Every desire should be deeply felt as all deeply felt mental actions become subconscious action,"

Mr. Larson said.

"I never realized how important directing desire was in one's life. In the beginning was desire, and now you mentioned the subconscious. What role does the subconscious play in the scheme of things?"

"Before I discuss the role we need to understand what the subconscious is. In defining the subconscious mind, it is first necessary to state that it is not a separate mind. There are not two minds. There is only one mind in man, but it has two phases; the conscious and the subconscious. We may define the conscious as the upper side of the mentality, and the subconscious as the under side. The subconscious may also be defined as a vast mental field permeating the entire objective personality, thereby filling every atom of the personality through and through. We shall come nearer the truth, however, if we think of the subconscious as a finer mental force, having distinct powers, functions and possibilities, or as a great mental sea of life, energy and power, the force and capacity of which has never been measured. Also, when a thought has been repeated in the mind for a sufficient amount of time it can become an intricate part of the subconscious mind," he said.

"It sounds like a progression; this new thought," Paul remarked.

"If people pattern their lives in a progressive manner they will ensure the success of their lives. We have stated that everything starts with desire; next plant the desire deep into the subconscious mind. The next step is incorporating right thinking which ushers in the power of concentration."

Mr. Larson took a sip of water, and continued, "When a man begins to think that he can apply the power of invention, his mind will begin to act upon the faculty of invention. The latent powers of this faculty will be aroused. These powers will accordingly be exercised more and more, and development will be promoted. This, however, is not all. Whenever the mind concentrates its attention upon a certain faculty, additional energy will be drawn into that faculty; thus power will be added to power, much will gather more, and as this may continue indefinitely there need be no end to the capacity and the ability that can be developed in that faculty."

Paul looked down at his notes, "Sir, you are speaking about positive thinking in overdrive."

Mr. Larson smiled, "When we think that we can, we must enter into the very soul of that thought and be thoroughly in earnest. It is in this manner that we awaken the finer creative energies of mind, those forces that build talent, ability and genius; those forces that make man great. We must be determined to do what we think we can do. This determination must be invincible, and must be animated with that depth of feeling that arouses all the powers of being into positive and united action. The power that we can do what we think we can do, will be placed at our command, and accordingly we may proceed successfully to do what we thought we could do."

Paul began to record the thoughts. "It is all coming together, the desire is planted in the subconscious mind which produces positive thoughts; those thoughts are strengthened with the ability for one to concentrate, right?" Paul asked.

"Yes, concentration is the ability to focus on one main purpose despite all the distractions. The purpose of concentration is to apply all the active forces of mind and personality upon that one thing which is being done now, and it may therefore be called the master key to all attainments and achievement. In its last analysis, the cause of all failure can be traced to the scattering of forces, and the cause of all achievement to the concentration of forces," Mr. Larson stated.

"What do you advise a person to do to achieve concentration?"

"The method is to train the mind to act in the subjective or psychological field; in other words, cause all thinking, all feeling and all action of thought, will and desire to become deeper and finer; in fact, deeper as far as possible all mental action. Whenever you concentrate or turn your attention upon any subject or object, try to feel deeply; try to think deeply, and try to turn thought into deeper realms of feeling."

"What is the outcome from all that work?" Paul asked.

"When you have developed that skill, you will begin to

act through undercurrents, and we are beginning to draw upon the immensity of that power that exists in the vast interior realms of our own mental world."

"Is there anything else that will assist us to become more optimistic?"

"Sure, we are far from done, but we are making progress. The next area feeds off the other traits we are discussing, and that is the power of will, or will power."

"I remember the words of Winston Churchill, 'Never give up!' "

"Whenever you exercise the will, try to place the action of that will as deeply in the world of your interior mental feeling as you possibly can; that is, do not originate will action on the surface, but in the depth of your own supreme individuality. Try to feel that it is the "I Am" that is exercising the power of the will, and then remember that the "I Am" lives constantly upon the supreme heights of absolute self-mastery. When you carry with you the inspiring thought constantly in your mind, you will carry the throne of the will, so to speak, farther and farther back into the interior realms of your greater mental world, higher and higher up into the ruling power of the supreme principle in mind."

Paul turned away. "You are an amazing man, Mr. Larson. How can the regular guy understand your wisdom?"

"When a person seeks growth in their life they create a magnetic field that attracts the information that they need. You can assist in their learning and understanding with your project," he added.

"You are right; I can break it down for people in small digestible parts to make learning easier."

"The next part in our progression of new thought is the development of character. Character is the proper direction of all things, and the proper use of all things in the human system. And the proper use of anything is that use that promotes the purpose for which that particular thing was created. To develop character it is therefore necessary to know what life is for, to know what actions promote that purpose of that life, and to know what actions retard that purpose. When the secret of right action is discovered, and every part of man is steadily trained in the expression of right action, character may be developed," Mr. Larson said.

"Character, why do people who have none seem to be able to succeed?"

"To distinguish between the right and the wrong becomes simplicity itself when one knows that the right promotes growth, while the wrong retards growth. Continuous advancement is the purpose of life; therefore, to live the right life is to live that life that promotes progress and growth, development and advancement in everything that pertains to life. For this reason, that action that promotes growth is in harmony with life itself, and must consequently be right, but that action that retards growth is at variance with life; therefore it is wrong; and wrong for that reason alone. Everything that promotes human advancement is right. Everything that interferes with human advancement is wrong. Here we have the basis of a system of ethics that is thoroughly complete, and so simple to live that no one need err in the least," Mr. Larson stated.

"We are coming full circle on the essence of our philosophy. Sir, I assume that all the gems of wisdom are not to be cashed in for material wealth."

"There is so much more to a person than materialism. The wealth of a person is not what they have, rather what they are. In the same way, people who are inclined to be materialistic could overcome that tendency entirely by concentrating attention constantly and thoroughly upon the idealistic side of life. In this case, those forces of the system that are perpetuation materialistic conditions would be transmuted into finer energies, and would thereby proceed to build up idealistic or more refined conditions of body, mind and personality."

"If I want to be become optimistic in my life, I would desire to be just that. I would have that desire seep deep into my subconscious mind which would produce right and positive thinking reinforced with concentration. Right concentrated thoughts would equip me with a strong stable will that would clothe my inner and outer self with a noble character. I believe this is the path to an optimistic existence." Paul said excitedly.

Christian Larson looked at Paul with a look of

compassion. "Say to yourself a hundred times every day, and mean it with all your heart: I will become more than I am. I will achieve more and more every day because I know that I can. I will recognize only that which is good in myself; only that which is good in others; only that in all things and places that I know should love and grow. When adversity threatens I will be more determined than ever in my life to prove that I can turn all things to good account. And when those whom I have trusted seem to fail me, I will have a thousand times more faith in the honor and nobleness of man. I will think only of that which has virtue and worth. I will wish only for that which can give freedom and truth. I will expect only that which can add to the welfare of the race. I will live to live more. I will speak to give encouragement, inspiration and joy. I will work to be of service to an ever-increasing number. And in every thought, word and action my ruling desire shall be, to enrich, ennoble and beautify existence for all who come my way."

The Lost Tenets of the Creed

The morning came early as Paul opened his eyes to check the time. It was 5:30am, so he rolled out of bed to start his day. He splashed some cold water on his face, and started a pot of coffee. He looked at the window to see the wind gusting. He remembered just a few months earlier the wind was a powerful weapon destructing everything in its path. Today, however, it just swayed the palm trees and kicked up the surf off the top of the waves. He was going through his notes. He couldn't wait to get back to the conversation with Christian Larson. Paul was puzzled for a moment. He carefully looked at the Creed in an old copy of Mr. Larson's book, *Your Forces and How to Use Them*, and then he compared it to the copy of the Creed given to him by the Optimist Club. There were two lines missing from his newer copy. He had used that newer version as a framework for his development of the philosophy of Optimism. The last missing lines stated:

> *To think well of yourself and to proclaim this fact to the world, not in loud words but in great deeds.*

> *To live in the faith that the whole world is on your side so long as you are true to the best that is in you.*

He was going to center the discussion on these tenets. He stretched out and then made himself a cup of coffee. Paul used to say that he liked his coffee black like his balance sheet, always in the black. He lay on his sofa and listened to the luring sounds of the waves crashing on the shore, and the occasional song of the seagulls as they flew by. His imagination was waking up and he saw the outline of Christian Larson standing in the doorway. "Come in sir, I wanted you to see the beauty that I am blessed with every morning."

Mr. Larson shook hands and sat down on the chair next to the sofa. "Yes, it is indeed beautiful. God's creations always are. What are you writing about for your project?" Mr. Larson asked.

"It is about the Philosophy of Optimism. You have been a tremendous source of inspiration for me personally, so I am very grateful that you would take time to visit with me," Paul said with admiration.

"I hope you will disclose the fact that to know God is the beginning of true wisdom." He looked directly at Paul.

Paul took another sip of coffee. "Would you like a cup?"

"Sure, I like just a little cream. Thank you."

"How about skim milk?" Paul asked. Mr. Larson nodded.

"It is interesting that when we were in the park together I read your creed, yet in the Optimist creed the last two tenets were not there. Do you know why?"

Mr. Larson shook his head. "I didn't even know 'til four year later that they were using my creed for their organization. Don't misunderstand me. I am glad that they like it, and that they are distributed all over the country. I did not receive any royalties. It was a very passive arrangement. I would go to the International Convention sometimes, and received some praise. It is a fine organization that does good work."

"Tell me about the tenets, and what you mean when you wrote, 'To think well of yourself and to proclaim this fact to the world, not in loud words but in great deeds'?"

Mr. Larson stood and walked to the patio door. He paused for a moment, turned and said, "To think well of yourself means to love yourself. What you love, you will respect; and what you respect you will value. The seeds of value are found in the wonder of love. It is biblical that, 'Love never fails.' If a person needs to make changes in their life for their improvement, the basic law of change must be taken into our own hands, and must be employed directly for producing the change we have in view; and to accomplish this love, nature must be so trained that we shall love only what we want to love, only what is greater and better than that which we have realized up to the present time. In this respect strong, highly developed souls will have no difficulty, because they have the power to see the great, the beautiful and the ideal in all things, but those who have not as yet acquired that power, must train their feeling with care, lest love frequently turns thought upon the low, the common or the ordinary."

"What you are saying is that love prepares us to act."

"Yes, when an individual incorporates love into their life the natural by product is character." Mr. Larson said.

"Character is what you do when no one can see you. How important is character to success?" Paul asked.

"Quite frankly, character is indispensable, no matter

what one's object in life may be. Character is the proper direction of all things and the proper use of all things in the human system. And the proper use of anything is that use that promotes the purpose for which that particular thing was created," Mr. Larson stated.

"So, character emerges in a person's life, what happens next?"

"The more brilliant and bright the character, the higher nature of the self; then it is man's nature to act because the soul of man is born. The greater the person's love, then the deeper the soul; when the soul is deepened then accomplishment is declared."

Paul wrote some notes on his pad. "What about the intention of the act?" he asked.

"The mere act is not sufficient, but rather the spirit that fuels the act is the answer. When you begin to help yourself, which means to make the best of what is in yourself; you begin to attract to yourself more and more of those helpful things that may exist all about you. In other words, constructive forces attract constructive forces; positive forces attract positive forces. A growing mind attracts elements and forces that help to promote growth, and people who are determined to make more and more of themselves, are drawn more and more into circumstances through which they will find the opportunity to make more of themselves. When a person has given their best, their world will open up and produce fruit."

Paul wrote feverishly. "Now the last tenet deals with a misunderstood concept called faith. How do you share the magical power of faith with others?" Paul asked earnestly.

"I wrote the phrase, 'To live in the faith that the whole world is on your side so long as you are true to the best that is in you' to remind people to interiorize faith. I am referring to a faith that not merely believes, but the faith that knows. With faith one can accomplish whatever they desire because faith will stay the course for victory. Faith is the hidden secret to everything, the key that unlocks every door that may exist in the universe; faith is the perfect way to that inner world from which all things proceed; faith is the royal path to the unbounded power, immeasurable wisdom and limitless love; faith is the gate ajar to that kingdom which first must be sought if all other things are to be added; faith is the hidden secret to every desire and need of man," Mr. Larson stated.

"What does a person do when they are not seeing the results of their faith?" Paul asked.

"The answer to the lack of faith is more faith; the solution to unfulfilled faith is abundant faith," he answered.

"How long should a person wait for the results?"

"You may not reach your results in the short term, but one must have continuous faith in reaching the goal. Never allow doubt, a stronghold in your mental makeup, but allow all the unbounded faith to deepen the soul. The outcome is a faith that is larger, stronger and greater than a person ever dreamed was possible in their life."

Paul, with his head buried in his notebook, looked up, and said, "The acting out of faith is a blessing in itself, isn't it?" Paul stumbled into profound thought.

"Yes, that is true, but our ideas and suggestions become alive with the enriching power of faith; furthermore, with the fullness of life and power when we also convey the real life or the real soul that is contained within the body of those thoughts. We have at such times entered the depths of mental life. We are beginning to act through undercurrents, and we are beginning to draw upon the immensity of that power that exists in the vast interior realms of our own mental world."

"I am in awe, sir; this information can radically change anyone's life in a meaningful way."

Christian Larson smiled at Paul. "The most important of all, however, is to live, think, and act in the absolute faith that the subconscious can and will do whatever it is directed to do. Faith is the hidden secret to everything; the key that unlocks every door that may exist in the universe; faith is the perfect way to that inner world from which all things proceed; faith is the royal path to the unbounded power, immeasurable wisdom and limitless love; faith is the gate ajar to that kingdom which first must be sought if all other things are to be added; faith is the hidden secret to every desire and need of man. This will cause truth to surface into the physical world where dreams become a reality. You are on the right track, so keep on keeping on."

Paul looked him straight in the eyes, and shook his hand. "Sir, I am going to make this project something very special because of this time spent with you, so I want to thank you for all that you do." Paul walked out of the meeting a changed man with a mission that burned in his soul.

The End/Your Beginning

James Rankin

Optimist International Member Invitation

Please type or print clearly

Name: _____

Were you ever a JOOI Member? ❑ Yes ❑ No   Are you currently a full-time college student? ❑ Yes ❑ No

HOME ADDRESS

Street: _____

City: _____ State/Province: _____ Zip/Postal Code: _____

Home Phone: _____ Fax: _____ E-mail : _____

BUSINESS ADDRESS

Firm Name: _____

Type of Business: _____

Street: _____

City: _____ State/Province: _____ Zip/Postal Code: _____

Business Phone: _____ E-mail : _____

Fax: _____ Business Position or Title: _____

May we contact you at work ❑ Yes ❑ No

YOUR SIGNATURE INDICATES YOUR ACCEPTANCE OF THIS INVITATION.

Signature: _____ Date: _____

Sponsor: _____

Optimist Club of _____

Dates approved by committee: _____ by Board of Directors: _____
Individuals who have committed sexual offenses against children may be denied membership and/or have their membership revoked.

Please complete and give to your local Optimist Club.

www.optimist.org

Order Form

If you would like a copy of the creed enlarged and suitable for framing, send $2.00 per copy plus $1.00 shipping and handling to:

Left Brain/ Right Brain Publishing, Inc.
9096 Jamaica Beach
Galveston, Texas 77554

Title	Price	QTY	Total
The Cherished Fruit	$18.00	_____	_____
The Source of the Shining	$21.95	_____	_____
The Philosopher Poet	$16.95	_____	_____
The Magic of Method Selling	$9.95	_____	_____
Living the Magic	$8.95	_____	_____
Mastering Method Management	$8.95	_____	_____
The Power of the Creed (original)	$8.00	_____	_____
The Power of the Creed (10th Anniversary Edition, Revised & Expanded)	$12.00	_____	_____
501 Tips for the Sales Professional	$8.95	_____	_____
Poems from the Spirit of Hope	$8.95	_____	_____
The Inner Renaissance Rediscovered	$8.95	_____	_____
Subtotals		_____	_____
Sales Tax (Texas residents only - 8.25%)			_____
Shipping ($2.00 per book)			_____
Total enclosed			_____

Name: _____

Company: _____

Address: _____

City, State & Zip: _____

Phone Number: _____

Contact james@lbrbpub.com for orders of 50+ books.
Quantity discounts apply.